HANDS-ON HISTOR[Y]
Projects and Activities to Accompan[y]

D0618492

TALES AND TREASURES
OF THE CALIFORNIA GOLD RUSH

Randall A. Reinstedt's
History & Happenings of California Series

Ghost Town Publications
P.O. Drawer 5998
Carmel, California 93921

10 9 8 7 6 5 4 3

Contributors

We gratefully acknowledge the contributions of the following friends and educators in the preparation of this **Hands-On History** teacher resource book:

Cynthia Bergez, Fourth GradeTeacher, Stuart Hall School for Boys, San Francisco
Donald R. Livermore, Librarian, Manzanita Elementary School, Seaside
Lisa Milligan, Fourth Grade Teacher, Ord Terrace Elementary School, Seaside
Kathy Nicholson, Librarian, La Mesa Elementary School, Monterey
Jane Snibbe, Librarian, Marshall Elementary School, Seaside
Patti Tai, Fourth Grade Teacher, La Mesa Elementary School, Monterey

Some clipart images from CorelDraw 5.0 were used in the preparation of this book.

Manufactured in the United States of America

ISBN 0-933818-65-3

Series Editor: *John Bergez*
Cover Illustration and Design: *Ed Greco*
Illustration on page 16: *B. Allen (Kip) Iliff*
Project Coordinator: *Debbie Reinstedt*
Typesetting, Design and Primary Project Development: *Erick and Mary Ann Reinstedt*

TEACHER TALK

Welcome to **Hands-On History!** In this resource book you will find a number of projects, activities, and ideas to help you integrate skills from across the curriculum as you teach the California Gold Rush. These activities cover the range between ready-to-use black line masters and in-depth activities that can occupy your class for several sessions.

Although these projects and activities can be used independently, they build on the themes in Randy Reinstedt's *Tales and Treasures of the California Gold Rush.* Randy's book covers all the essentials of the Gold Rush while recounting fascinating tales of treasure, lost gold, practical jokes, outlaws, and entertainers—all told with the vividness that is characteristic of each of his books in the **History & Happenings of California Series.**

Getting Started

This **Hands-On History** book is divided into three sections plus a Readers' Theatre. At the start of each section you will find Teacher's Notes and instructions for all of the section's activities. The Teacher's Notes include:

✧ The page number of the student pages for the activity
✧ An overview of the activity
✧ A list of materials
✧ Directions for putting the activity into action
✧ Extension ideas

You might want to make a folder for each activity in which you can keep copies of the instructions, the activity, your own notes, and any supplemental material.

Be sure to review the student pages before reading the "Directions" portion of Teacher's Notes. Instructions that are on the student pages are not repeated in Teacher's Notes. References to the "text" throughout this book refer to Randy Reinstedt's *Tales and Treasures of the California Gold Rush.*

Hands-On History at a Glance

Section 1: Discovering the Gold Rush

This section's activities stress who came to the gold fields, the different routes they used to make their journey, and what techniques they used to get the gold once they arrived.

Section 2: Life in a Mining Town

This section's activities cover the spectrum of Gold Country life. Although these activities can each be used independently, the Teacher's Notes present ideas on how to use them in combination to re-create a mining town in your classroom.

Section 3: The Lure and Lore of Gold

This section's activities integrate the teaching of skills from across the curriculum while building on the theme of gold and the California Gold Rush.

Readers' Theatre

The Readers' Theatre script presents an exciting Gold Rush "whodunit" in the form of a courtroom drama for students to perform.

An answer key for all activities that require a "set" answer is located in the back of the book. The inside front cover shows a curriculum chart that will help you to quickly pick activities that meet your requirements of subjects and skills to cover. Where applicable, the chart also lists the corresponding chapters in *Tales and Treasures of the California Gold Rush.* These chapters provide historical background and context for the activities.

Ideas to Try

✧ Assign "individual" activities like Westward Journey Word Match and The Lucky Miner Mine to cooperative teams or groups, especially if you anticipate that some students may have difficulty completing an activity.

✧ Assign point values in units of "gold" to the different activities. (Bags of gold with different "point" values are available for you to copy at the end of Teacher Talk.) As the students complete the activities, they col-

Hands-On History: Tales & Treasures of the California Gold Rush   Copyright 1995 • Ghost Town Publications • Carmel, California

lect "gold" to exchange for goods at a "general store" (stocked with food items, party favors, small school supplies, etc.). Or . . .

✧ Stage a "white elephant" auction at the end of the Gold Rush unit. Have students bring unwanted objects from their homes for the auction. At the auction, they make bids using the "gold" they have earned during the unit.

✧ Create graphs showing the dollar value of your students' holdings of "gold." If you award "gold" in ounces, you can convert the students' gold units into dollar amounts using the current price of gold from the newspaper. Update the graph each day/week as the price of gold changes and students' holdings increase.

✧ Set up and decorate stations around classroom (Town Square, Gambling Hall, Mining Camp, Newspaper Office, General Store, Theatre, etc.). Label the stations with appropriate signs. You might even create false fronts in front of the "buildings." Present and display the different activities in the station that best fits them.

✧ Showcase your students' work by having a Gold Rush Jamboree in which you invite students from other classes, teachers, or parents into your class. During the jamboree your students could teach their guests to pan for gold and play games of chance. They can dress up as miners, tell stories about how Gold Rush towns got their names, sing miner songs, and present the Readers' Theatre and Miners' Court—all to a backdrop of your class newspapers, signs, laws, journals, and other exciting projects.

Be sure to check out the exciting "Gold Nuggets" of information that are scattered both throughout the book and in More Gold Nuggets (pages 62-63). We hope you and your students enjoy the wealth of projects and activities in this book. Write us and let us know!

The Ghost Town Family

John Bergez, Series Editor
Randy, Debbie, Erick, and Mary Ann Reinstedt

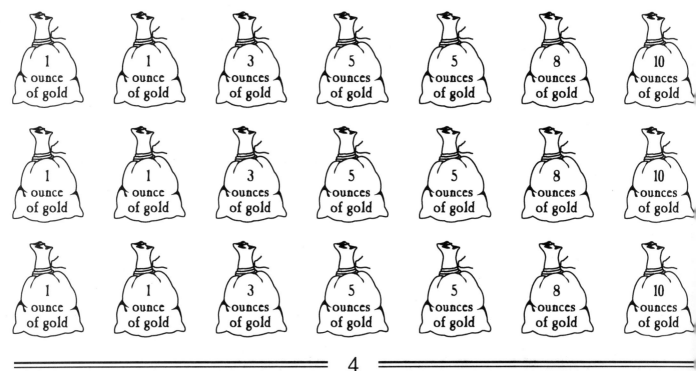

RELATED READINGS

Encourage your students to explore the California Gold Rush by reading some of the following stories and factual books. This resource list includes stories suitable for fourth graders and books that teachers will find useful for background information and illustrations.

Chambers, Catherine. CALIFORNIA GOLD RUSH: SEARCH FOR TREASURE. *In California in 1848 two brothers helping to build a sawmill for John Sutter witness the discovery of gold and decide to stake a claim for themselves.*

Coerr, Eleanor. CHANG'S PAPER PONY. *In San Francisco during the 1850s, Chang wants a pony but cannot have one.*

Donahue, Marilyn Cram. STRAIGHT ALONG A CROOKED ROAD. *As her family travels from Vermont to settle in California in the early 1850s fourteen-year-old Luanna learns to accept life for what it is, no matter where.*

Fleischman, Sid. BY THE GREAT HORN SPOON. *This exciting 1849 adventure features a journey to California by ship. A 10-year-old boy and the loyal family butler race against time to strike paydirt in the Gold Rush and return to save the family home in Boston.*

Flory, Jane. THE GOLDEN VENTURE. *Minnie stows away on her father's wagon, heading west from Missouri to California to join the Gold Rush. While the search for gold goes on, Minnie has many adventures of her own in wild and woolly San Francisco.*

Harvey, Brett. CASSIE'S JOURNEY: GOING WEST IN THE 1860's. *A young girl relates the hardships and dangers of traveling with her family in a covered wagon from Illinois to California during the 1860s.*

Hoobler, Dorothy. TREASURE IN THE STREAM: THE STORY OF A GOLD RUSH GIRL. *When Amy Harris's family is caught up in the discovery of gold close to their farm in California, their lives change forever.*

Lake, A. GOLD FEVER. *This book describes the origins, the individuals, and the results of the California Gold Rush that began in 1848.*

Lampman, Evelyn Sibley. THE BANDIT OF MOK HILL. *This historical fiction tale tells of a young boy's desire to join the Murrieta gang. Many of the problems that faced the people of the Gold Rush are brought out.*

Laurgaad, Rachel Kelly. PATTY REED'S DOLL. *Based on the actual happenings in the fateful Donner crossing of the Sierras in 1846. This pre-Gold Rush tale is told through the eyes of a small wooden doll who traveled from Illinois to California in Patty Reed's pocket.*

Hands-On History: Tales & Treasures of the California Gold Rush   Copyright 1995 • Ghost Town Publications • Carmel, California

McNeer, Mary. THE CALIFORNIA GOLD RUSH: LANDMARK. *Includes true tales of the Gold Rush, slightly dramatized. These stories help bring the happenings and characters of the Gold Rush to life.*

Reinstedt, Randall A. ONE-EYED CHARLEY, THE CALIFORNIA WHIP. *This fictional retelling of the true story of an authentic Gold Rush hero brings the incredible tale of stagecoach driver Charley Parkhurst to young readers in a way that will keep them enthralled and reading. As they hear of Charley's heroics and the remarkable secret discovered following "his" death, they learn that women—and girls—can be just as brave and resourceful as the hardiest of men.*

Rounds, Glen. SWEET BETSY FROM PIKE. *Betsy and Ike, from Pike, endure the hardships of the trip west during the California Gold Rush. Based on the folk song.*

Wade, Linda. CALIFORNIA: THE RUSH FOR GOLD. *This book describes the discovery of gold in California and its impact on the development of California and the West.*

Williams, Lucy. THE AMERICAN WEST. *Surveys the history of the American West, covering such aspects as the native inhabitants, the first European settlers, the cowboys and the Gold Rush.*

DISCOVERING THE GOLD RUSH

✧ Where in the World Did I Come From?

✧ Westward Journey Word Match

✧ Wagons to California Game

✧ Betcha-Can'ts

✧ How Did They Get That Gold?

The discovery of gold quickly made California's rugged Sierra Nevada the destination for people from throughout the world, including the United States. In this section you can explore the rush to California with word searches and word matches, involve your students in the westward movement with the Wagons to California board game, and challenge them to use different reference sources and skills with Betcha-Can'ts. Finally, explore the different gold-mining techniques by making an information wheel and using it to answer questions.

Where in the World Did I Come From? (pg. 9)

Overview: Word search showing different countries from which people came to California. Teaches geographic facts.

Directions

1. If the approach on the student page is too difficult for some of your students, reverse the process and have them find the names of the countries in the word search and then figure out which question they belong to.

2. Students may use the text, encyclopedias, atlases, maps, and other reference materials to find the answers.

Extension

1. Assign students a country from which prospectors came and have them research the country (e.g., geographic location, customs, clothing, food) and tell the class about it, and their journey to California from it. You may want to have them make their presentations during a "Where Did I Come From?" day. Put a world map on the wall and have

students place a marker on the country they are "from." Have them use a made-up name, typical of their country. They can also bring in a food from their country's region, wear traditional costumes, and perform skits, songs, and dances to share with the class.

Westward Journey Word Match (pg. 10)

Overview: Word match dealing with three main routes (Overland, Cape Horn, Panama) used to travel to California. Use as a follow-up to a discussion of how prospectors got to the gold fields.

Directions

1. If this word match is too difficult, have students look up the words in the list on the right first and then try to match that information to the correct question, using a process of elimination. The most benefit will be gained if you follow up this activity with a

discussion of each question.

2. Students may use the text, encyclopedias, atlases, maps and other reference materials to find the answers.

Extension

1. Students write a story using each of the answer words for the 10 questions (the story can be funny or serious).

Wagons to California Game (pp. 11-12)

Overview: Board game highlighting adversities of westward overland travel. Requires students to choose between risky and safe routes.

Materials: 1 die and 1 board per group; 1 marker per student

Directions

1. Copy 1 game board per group. Enlarge the board on a copier if possible to make play easier for larger groups. Students may want

---

7

Teacher's Notes (continued)

to color the boards, or you may want to laminate them and reuse them year after year.

2. Break class into groups of 2-5 students.

3. Students may use coins, peas, beans, or other small objects as markers.

4. Before beginning, review the rules with the class and discuss conservative *vs.* risky choices and the influence of good *and* bad luck.

Extensions

1. Brainstorm with your students good and bad events that could have happened to westward travelers. Discuss the relative importance of each and turn them into your own class "LUCK" box. Put this on the board and have students play the game again using it.

2. Using the idea above, make LUCK decks. Put different ideas and results (i.e., forward 3, back 2, etc.) on 3 x 5-inch cards and have the students draw from the deck when they land on a LUCK space.

3. Have students make notes on the situations they encountered on their westward journey while playing the game (what terrain they passed through, who they passed or met along the way, good and bad luck, if they even completed their journey, etc.). Then have them write a letter to family or a friend back home telling about their trip. The students may even want to make a journal of their westward experiences.

4. Students love to beat the teacher! Put the board game onto a transparency and place it on an overhead projector. Have one marker for yourself and one for the class. Play against the class, either choosing a representative from the class to roll the die or letting the students take turns rolling. As you move through the board, use the different events as springboards for discussion.

Betcha-Can'ts (pp. 13-14)

Overview: Challenging Gold Rush-oriented questions for students to answer that utilize many different skills from across the curriculum.

Materials: Writing paper

Directions

1. Students may use the text, encyclopedias, atlases, maps, and other reference materials to find the answers.

How Did They Get That Gold? (pp. 15-18)

Overview: A science and art project in which students make a mining techniques information wheel to use in answering questions.

Materials: Writing paper, scissors, glue, tagboard (if you choose to mount the wheels on a stiff backing), and round head fasteners to attatch the wheels together

Directions

1. Copy pages 15 and 16 back to back. Copy pages 17 and 18 on separate pieces of paper.

2. Have students construct their wheels and use them to answer the questions on page 15 on a separate sheet of paper. Then have them use the wheel to fill in the blanks on page 16.

Extensions

1. Discuss the environmental effects of different mining techniques, especially hydraulic mining. Students could research the different environmental effects of mining before this discussion. (See Gold Nugget on this page.)

2. Discuss the transition of gold seeking from lone prospectors to huge businesses.

3. Use this activity to lead into Panning for Gold, page 29.

GOLD NUGGET

The waste from hydraulic mining washed down out of the Sierra Nevada and clogged rivers, leading to extensive flooding and the disruption of farmlands and agriculture. One orchard was covered with twenty feet of waste. Thousands of acres of farmlands were buried, and the waste even discolored San Francisco Bay. Hydraulic mining continued to be used until the 1880s when it was prohibited by law unless the waste could be disposed of. This was nearly impossible, so the method ceased being used through most of the Gold Country.

Hands-On History: Tales & Treasures of the California Gold Rush   Copyright 1995 ◆ Ghost Town Publications ◆ Carmel, California

WHERE IN THE WORLD DID I COME FROM?

After the initial discovery of gold in 1848, prospectors from all across the United States and the world flooded into California. By 1850 about eight out of every ten people in California had arrived during the Gold Rush!

Read the clues to help you find the names of some of the countries that prospectors came from. Use an atlas, encyclopedia, and other reference books for help. After you read a clue, circle the name of the country in the word search and then write that name in the correct blank. Search forward, backward, up, down, and diagonally. Good luck!

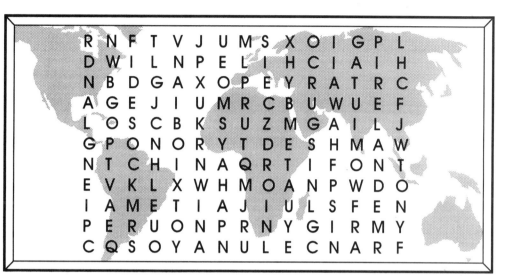

```
R N F T V J U M S X O I G P L
D W I L N P E L I H C I A I H
N B D G A X O P E Y R A T R C
A G E J I U M R C B U W U E F
L O S C B K S U Z M G A I L J
G P O N O R Y T D E S H M A W
N T C H I N A Q R T I F O N T
E V K L X W H M O A N P W D O
I A M E T I A J I U L S F E N
P E R U O N P R N Y G I R M Y
C Q S O Y A N U L E C N A R F
```

Clues

1. Where I am from we are famous for a boat called a *junk*. California is directly east of my country along latitude 40° north with only present-day Japan and Korea in between.

2. South of Denmark, my country borders the North and Baltic Seas.

3. When it is summer in California it is winter where I come from. My country is long and thin, and our name sounds like a food. Ships traveling to California around Cape Horn would have passed my country.

4. My country is famous for an animal that jumps and carries its young in a pouch. Many people during the Gold Rush thought we were all a bunch of convicts.

5. My country is to the west of the mainland of Europe and our police are called Bobbies. The Tower of London is located there.

6. My country is an island just west of #5, and we are famous for potatoes.

7. My country's capital is Lima. We are on the western coast of South America.

8. Where I am from is an island. It has been a state since 1959—in fact it was the 50th state to join the union.

9. My country's capital is Paris. One of our famous leaders from the past was Napoleon.

10. I speak Spanish and come from a neighboring country of California. The intersection of latitude 20° north and longitude 100° west occurs in my country.

Miner's Name: _____

WESTWARD JOURNEY WORD MATCH

Explore the different routes gold seekers chose to get to the gold fields of California as you complete the questions on this page.

Read each sentence on the left. Then, from the list on the right, find the word that completes that sentence. Use your Gold Rush book, a dictionary, an atlas, and other reference materials for help. Then, write the letter of the correct word in the blank next to the sentence it completes. (HINT: You won't use all the words in the list on the right because there are more words than sentences.)

_____ 1. For travelers taking the overland route, the best time to leave was in _____, so they had plenty of feed for the animals and fewer risks of snow-blocked passes.

_____ 2. The most popular sea route to California from the east coast of the United States was the _____ voyage.

_____ 3. The distance from St. Joseph, Missouri to San Francisco, California as the crow flies (the straight line distance from one point to another) is about _____ miles. (HINT: Find a map with a scale and measure the distance using a straight edge. Then find the closest number on the list to your number.)

_____ 4. _____ was a common life-threatening disease that argonauts feared when traveling by land or sea. On the overland route, this disease was often found in contaminated water holes.

_____ 5. The last treacherous mountain range the prospectors traveling overland had to cross before reaching the gold fields was the _____.

_____ 6. The voyage for ships sailing from the East Coast around Cape Horn might take _____ months or longer.

_____ 7. Two of the main communities where people would gather to begin their journey to the California gold fields in groups are in Missouri. They are St. Joseph and _____. (HINT: Its name is the theme of the Fourth of July celebration.)

_____ 8. Even though travelers might find water along their route, not all was drinkable. The common problem with the water was a high level of *alkali*, which is a type of _____.

_____ 9. The Isthmus of Panama is a narrow strip of land that connects the North and South American continents and was crossed to get from the _____ Sea to the Pacific Ocean.

_____ 10. _____ were not as fast as mules when crossing the country, but they were stronger, more reliable, and could eat food that mules wouldn't.

A. Sierra Nevada

B. 1500

C. oxen

D. 18

E. cholera

F. spring

G. 6

H. Cape Town

I. Black

J. Freedom

K. sheep

L. Independence

M. September

N. cancer

O. 2600

P. Caribbean

Q. Cape Horn

R. Rocky Mountains

S. salt

T. coprolite

_____

GOLD NUGGET

Indian attacks did not become a serious problem for westward travelers until after the peak Gold Rush years (1849-1852).

Hands-On History: Tales & Treasures of the California Gold Rush

Copyright 1995 • Ghost Town Publications • Carmel, California

Miner's Name: _____

WAGONS TO CALIFORNIA GAME

Overland travel to California during the Gold Rush was a risky venture. Making the trip successfully might have been determined by a single stroke of good or bad luck. Try your luck as you head to the gold fields and remember, you can't find gold if you don't get there in the first place . . .

What You Need: (1) One six-sided die; (2) one marker per player; (3) a game board.

Objective: To be the first player to arrive at the gold fields (FINISH).

To Start: Roll a die to see who goes first. The person with the highest number starts and play then passes to the left.

To Play

1. The players take turns rolling the die and moving their markers. Before rolling the die for the first time you must announce which route you are taking to the gold fields. *You may not change your mind once you have rolled.* Route Safe is longer, but it has fewer possible problems that could delay you. Route Risky is shorter, but it has more chances for dangerous and costly delays.

2. Continue taking turns rolling the die and moving your markers until one player reaches the gold fields (FINISH). If on your last roll you roll a higher number than you need to land on FINISH, you win! You don't need to roll an exact count.

3. If you end your turn on a black space (⬡), follow the instructions next to the space.

4. Luck (both good and bad) was very important in the westward journey. If you end your turn on a LUCK space, roll the die again. Match the number that you rolled to the same number in the LUCK box at the bottom of the game board, and follow the instructions next to that number.

NOTE: More than one marker may occupy the same space.

GOLD NUGGETS

During the 1850s gold rush in Australia, a wagon wheel accidentally turned up a huge gold nugget weighing more than 150 pounds!

Pure gold is one of the softest metals and the easiest metal to work into different shapes. A single ounce of gold can be drawn into a wire more than 40 miles long!

Hands-On History: Tales & Treasures of the California Gold Rush   Copyright 1995 • Ghost Town Publications • Carmel, California

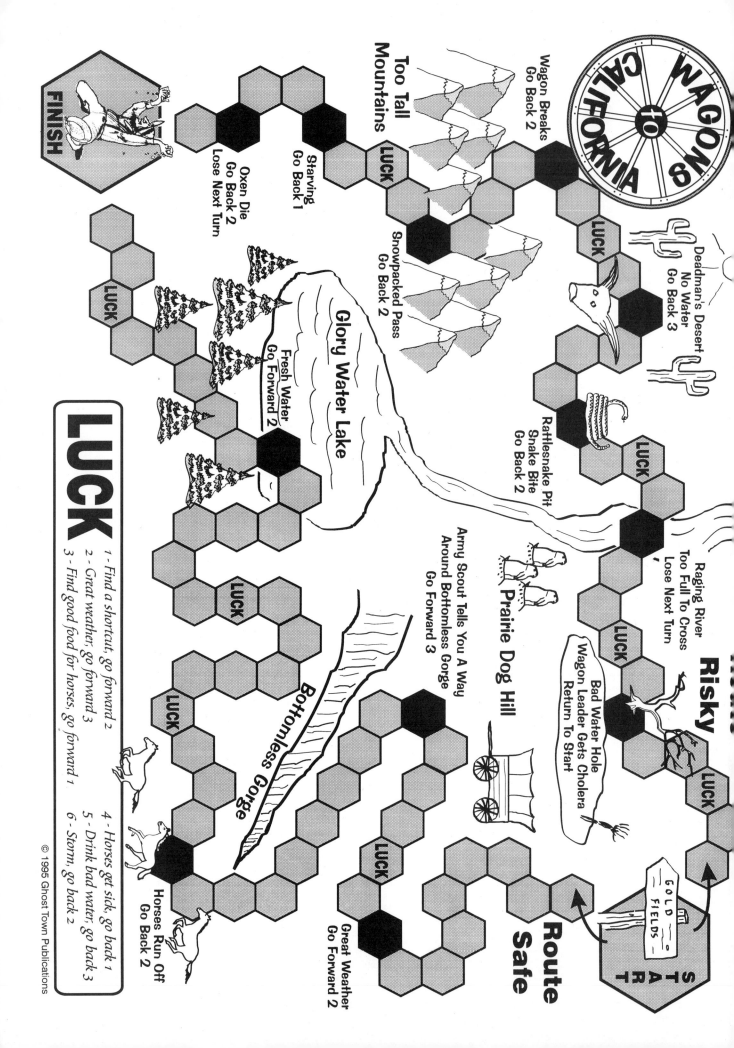

WAGONS to CALIFORNIA

Wagon Breaks
Go Back 2

Too Tall Mountains

LUCK

Snowpacked Pass
Go Back 2

Starving
Go Back 1

Oxen Die
Go Back 2
Lose Next Turn

FINISH

Deadman's Desert
No Water
Go Back 3

LUCK

Rattlesnake Pit
Snake Bite
Go Back 2

LUCK

Glory Water Lake

Fresh Water
Go Forward 2

LUCK

Raging River
Too Full To Cross
Lose Next Turn

LUCK

Risky

Bad Water Hole
Wagon Leader Gets Cholera
Return To Start

Army Scout Tells You A Way
Around Bottomless Gorge
Go Forward 3

Prairie Dog Hill

LUCK

LUCK

Bottomless Gorge

Horses Run Off
Go Back 2

LUCK

LUCK

GOLD FIELDS

START

Route Safe

Great Weather
Go Forward 2

LUCK

1 - Find a shortcut, go forward 2
2 - Great weather, go forward 3
3 - Find good food for horses, go forward 1
4 - Horses get sick, go back 1
5 - Drink bad water, go back 3
6 - Storm, go back 2

© 1995 Ghost Town Publications

BETCHA-CAN'TS

Can you or your team score 100 points? Betchacan't!

> Finding the answers to the following questions about the California Gold Rush may in-
> volve a little research. To answer them, you'll have to do some research in your
> classroom or school library. In addition to the book *Tales and Treasures of the California
> Gold Rush*, use atlases, maps, encyclopedias, and other reference books.
>
> Pretend you're a detective, and see whether you can find all the answers. Each answer is
> worth the number of points shown. Good luck!

1. OK, let's start with an easy one to get you warmed up. What was the real name of Gold Rush outlaw Rattlesnake Dick? (Got your *Tales and Treasures of the California Gold Rush*? Try the index) Too easy? Well, one source says that Rattlesnake Dick had wanted to be known as the "_____ *of the Placers."* What is the missing word? All right, smarty. Rattlesnake Dick's gang robbed a *mule* train in what was one of the biggest robberies of the Gold Rush. What is the difference between a horse and a mule? You have to get all three of these . . . **(10 points)**

2. Many years ago, the United States Government started keeping a huge store of gold bars to back up the money it printed. (Without the government's gold to back it up, the money would only be worth the paper it was printed on!) Each of the government's gold bars weighs 28 pounds. How heavy is that? To find out, figure out about how many of these bars of gold it would take to equal your own weight. **(5 points)**

3. Speaking of the government's gold, can you find out why a place called Fort Knox is famous? (Got an encyclopedia handy?) **(10 points)**

4. California's Highway 49 is a famous route through the Gold Country. Suppose you wanted to take a tour along this scenic highway from Columbia to Auburn. Would the distance you travel be closer to 75 miles, 100 miles, or 125 miles? (Guess you need a road map, huh? Maybe the little numbers printed alongside the highway can help you with the answer to this question.) **(10 points)** Now suppose you average 40 miles per hour on your trip. About how long will it take you to get from Columbia to Auburn? **(5 points)**

5. The words "gold" and "golden" appear in the names of many things besides gold, including *goldilocks* (a plant) and *golden retriever* (a kind of dog). Can you find out three more things that have "gold" or "golden" in their names? (Let's see . . . What kind of book is organized in a way that you can look up words that start with "gold" or "golden"?) **(5 points)** For another 5 points, can you explain *why* each of your items has "gold" in its name? **(5 points)**

Golden Retriever

6. Say, did you know that one standard-sized paper clip weighs 1 gram? Well, here's an easy one. If you put a nickel on one side of a balance scale and 5 paper clips on the other and the scale balances, then how many grams does a nickel weigh? **(5 points)** Now, this is a little tougher. If you used nickels and the balance scale to weigh gold, how many nickels would you need to equal 2 kilograms? (HINT: You first have to figure out how many grams are in a kilogram.) **(10 points)**

7. Gold is a *pure* metal (it is not made up of any other metals). Other examples of pure metals are copper and tin. Unlike pure metals, *alloys* are mixtures of metals that have been melted and blended together. Two common alloys are brass and bronze. (You may have objects made up of these alloys in your home.) For 10 points, can you find out what metals are blended to make each of these two alloys? **(10 points)**

8. Did you know a cubic yard of gravel is as much gravel as you could put in a box that is 1 yard long, 1 yard wide, and 1 yard high? A miner could pan ½ a cubic yard of gravel a day. Two miners, using a rocker, could go through 1½ cubic yards of gravel a day. So, how many more cubic yards a day could two miners with a rocker go through than two miners panning? **(5 points)** At the end of 5 days of looking for gold, how many more cubic yards of gravel would two men with a rocker go through than two men panning? **(5 points)**

9. Many people learned of the gold discovery in California through newspaper stories. If you were a newspaper reporter, how would you "break the news" of this exciting event? Write a paragraph giving the most important details of the discovery. Be sure to include the "four w's" of a good news article—*who, what, where,* and *when.* Don't forget to give your news story a big headline! **(15 points)**

Miner's Name: _____

HOW DID THEY GET THAT GOLD?

Gold! The story of the California Gold Rush is the story of fortune-seekers' creative attempts to gather this elusive treasure. Two main types of gold deposits were sought: LODE and PLACER (defined on your information wheel). Deposits of placer gold were easier to find and to work. As these deposits were depleted, the techniques for finding the remaining gold became more expensive and difficult. More and more, the hunt for gold became a big business rather than an adventure for a single prospector with a gold pan.

Directions

1. Cut out and make your Gold Rush Mining Techniques Wheel, following the directions on the two pages.

2. Use the wheel and the information above to answer the questions below on a separate piece of paper.

3. After you have answered the questions, turn to the next page. Use your wheel to fill in the blanks in the sentences.

Questions

1. List three different mining methods used to find placer deposits.

2. What is the major difference between lode deposits and placer deposits?

3. Which mining technique was likely to be used to wash gold from the side of a mountain?

4. What type of equipment was used to locate lode deposits by quartz mining?

5. What was the easiest method for removing loose gold from rock, sand, and gravel?

6. Why was mining in a Coyote Hole a dangerous job?

7. What part do both a Long Tom and a Rocker have in common for catching gold?

☆ **BONUS QUESTION:** Which two techniques are most likely to require more money and people than a one or two miner team could provide?

GOLD NUGGET

✧ The largest gold mine in the United States is the Homestake Mine in Lead, South Dakota. This mine has reached a depth of more than 6,000 feet (more than a mile)!

✧ A shaft of one gold mine in South Africa descends more than 12,000 feet (more than two miles) into the Earth!

Hands-On History: Tales & Treasures of the California Gold Rush

1. A dry river bed was a good place to make a _____ hole. By sinking a hole down to the _____, a miner could bring up soil that contained the _____ (lode or placer?) deposits that had settled through the shifting of the earth.

2. Mine shafts sunk deep underground into these hills would most likely be looking for _____ (lode or placer?) deposits. This is called _____ mining and it usually required a lot of men and money.

3. If enough water could be diverted to build up pressure, this slope could quickly be washed away down to sluices using the technique of _____.

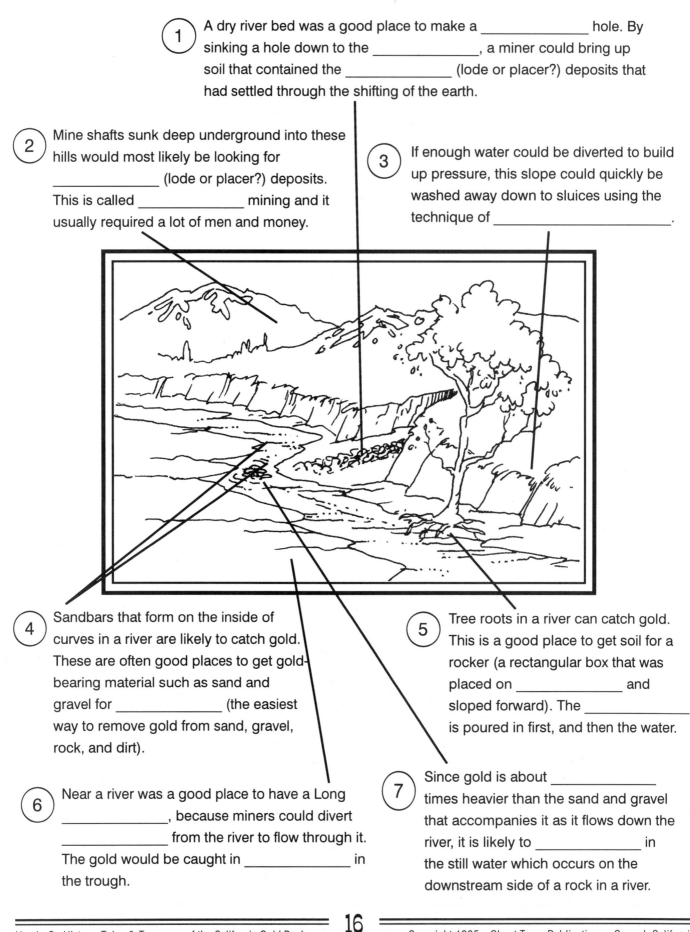

4. Sandbars that form on the inside of curves in a river are likely to catch gold. These are often good places to get gold-bearing material such as sand and gravel for _____ (the easiest way to remove gold from sand, gravel, rock, and dirt).

5. Tree roots in a river can catch gold. This is a good place to get soil for a rocker (a rectangular box that was placed on _____ and sloped forward). The _____ is poured in first, and then the water.

6. Near a river was a good place to have a Long _____, because miners could divert _____ from the river to flow through it. The gold would be caught in _____ in the trough.

7. Since gold is about _____ times heavier than the sand and gravel that accompanies it as it flows down the river, it is likely to _____ in the still water which occurs on the downstream side of a rock in a river.

Hands-On History: Tales & Treasures of the California Gold Rush

Gold Rush Mining Techniques Wheel (page 1)

1. If you are going to glue the two pieces that make up your wheel onto tagboard, do that first.
2. Cut out the large wheel on this page. This is your backing wheel.
3. Cut out the smaller wheel on page 2. This will be the front of your completed wheel.
4. Carefully cut out the two windows on the smaller wheel.
5. Center the small wheel on top of the large wheel.
6. Push a fastener through the center of the two wheels. Fasten it in back. (Your teacher will give you a fastener.)
7. You are now ready to use your Gold Rush Mining Techniques Wheel.

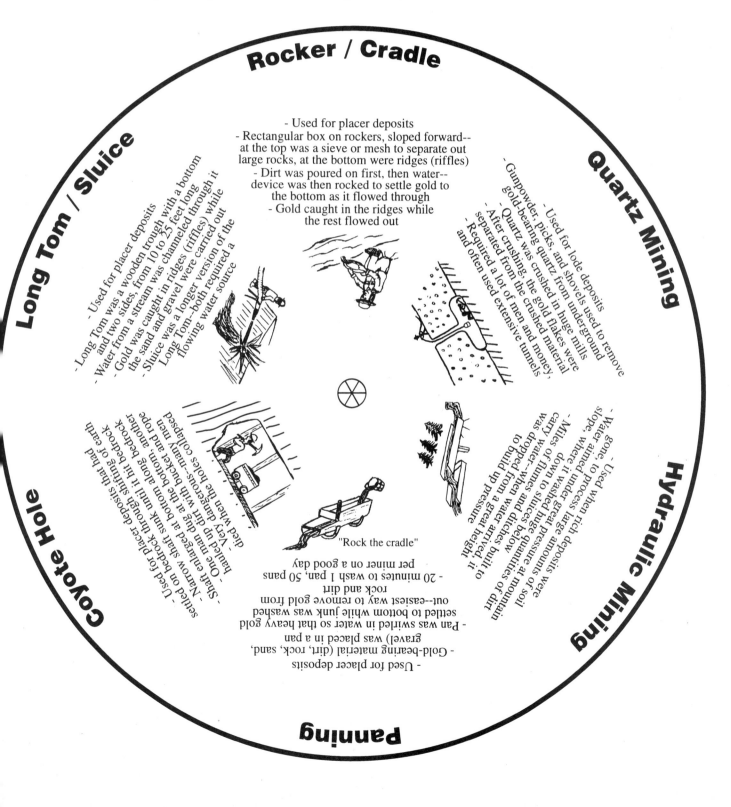

Rocker / Cradle

- Used for placer deposits
- Rectangular box on rockers, sloped forward--
at the top was a sieve or mesh to separate out
large rocks, at the bottom were ridges (riffles)
- Dirt was poured on first, then water--
device was then rocked to settle gold to
the bottom as it flowed through
- Gold caught in the ridges while
the rest flowed out

"Rock the cradle"

Quartz Mining

- Used for lode deposits
- Gunpowder, picks, and shovels used to remove
gold bearing quartz from underground
- Quartz was crushed in huge mills
- After crushing, the gold flakes were
separated from the crushed material
- Required a lot of men and money,
and often used extensive tunnels

Long Tom / Sluice

- Used for placer deposits
- Long Tom was a wooden trough with a bottom
and two sides, from 10 to 25 feet long
- Water from a stream was channeled through it
- Gold was caught in ridges (riffles) while
the sand and gravel were carried out
- Sluice was a longer version of the
Long Tom--both required a
flowing water source

Coyote Hole

- Used for placer deposits that settled on bedrock
- Shaft sunk until it hit bedrock
- Quartz enlarged at the bottom along another
- Very dangerous--many men
died when the holes collapsed
- Narrow shaft dug through the head
of earth with bucket and rope

Hydraulic Mining

- Used when rich deposits
were under great amounts of soil
- Water aimed at a mountain
slope, where it washed away dirt
- Miles of flumes and ditches built to
carry water--water arrived,
was dropped from a great height
to build up pressure

Panning

- Used for placer deposits
- Gold-bearing material (dirt, rock, sand,
gravel) was placed in a pan
- Pan was swirled in water so that heavy gold
settled to bottom while junk was washed
out--easiest way to remove gold from
rock and dirt
- 20 minutes to wash 1 pan, 50 pans
per miner on a good day

Gold Rush Mining Techniques Wheel (page 2)

1. To use your new Gold Rush Mining Techniques Wheel, turn the small wheel until the large window is directly under the name of the mining technique you are interested in learning about.

2. When the window and the name are lined up, the words in the large window will tell about that technique. The small window will show a picture of it.

3. Don't forget to read all of the information on the front of your wheel. It will give you information about gold in general that will help you to understand the different techniques.

GOLD NUGGET

When the miners said they were separating the gold from the "dirt," the "dirt" they were talking about might actually be made up of dirt, sand, gravel, rock, and more. Often their use of the word "dirt" meant whatever wasn't gold.

Cut out this window

Gold Rush Mining Techniques Wheel

LODE Deposits

Gold that is moving up to the Earth's surface in veins is called LODE gold. Miners had to use tunnels or mines to get this gold. (A vein is a lengthy occurrence of gold beneath the surface of the Earth.)

PLACER Deposits

Lode gold that has reached the Earth's surface and been eroded by water and wind is called PLACER gold. Placer gold is usually found in ancient river beds and at the bottom of flowing streams. Often it is flakes and dust, but sometimes it is nuggets. The techniques used to get placer gold all depend on the heaviness of gold. For instance, gold settles to the bottom of a miner's pan because it is about 8 times heavier than the sand and gravel it is mixed with.

Cut out this window

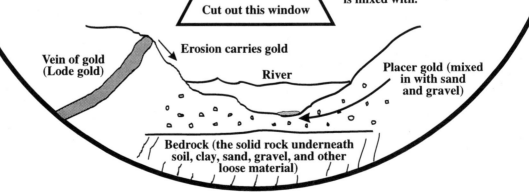

Erosion carries gold

Vein of gold (Lode gold)

River

Placer gold (mixed in with sand and gravel)

Bedrock (the solid rock underneath soil, clay, sand, gravel, and other loose material)

LIFE IN A MINING TOWN

- ✧ Start Your Own Gold Rush Town
- ✧ Buying and Selling, Gold Rush Style
- ✧ Panning for Gold
- ✧ Music to a Miner's Ears
- ✧ Tell Me a Wild One

- ✧ Miners' Court
- ✧ Wanted!
- ✧ Shut the Box
- ✧ 49er
- ✧ Get the News Out!

This section provides all you need to create your own mining town in your classroom. In these activities students choose their town's name and establish its laws, explore the laws of supply and demand in an exciting game of merchants and miners, try their luck at gold panning, and sing and make music in a miner's pick-up band. They write an ending to a story of how a Gold Rush town got its name, explore Gold Country justice in a mock trial, make a wanted poster of a real Gold Rush outlaw, play games of chance that miners might have played in their time off, and edit and publish their town's newspaper.

You can pick and choose among these activities according to your needs and schedule. Taken together, however, these activities cover the spectrum of life in the gold fields and will allow your students to establish and "take ownership" of their own Gold Rush town. To set the scene for the activities that take place in and around your "town," consider establishing stations in your classroom. By running some activities concurrently, you can avoid the problem of needing to find a gold panning bucket for every 3 or 4 children in your class, etc. Decorate the stations and give them creative names. For example, one corner of your classroom could be the Mining Camp where students pan for gold. Another station could be the Gambling Hall where they try their luck at games of chance. For other activities, the whole classroom could become a "Town Square." The more students can immerse themselves in their roles as miners and townspeople, the richer the experience will be.

Start Your Own Gold Rush Town (pp. 23-24)
(Name Your Town / Make Laws for Your Town / Decorate Your Town)
Overview: Students establish a town/mining camp, choose a town name and the story behind it, and make both Gold Rush laws and "laws" to govern their behavior during

subsequent activities. Finally, the town comes to life with signs and banners.
Materials: Material for signs (cardboard, pens, paints, etc.)
Directions for Name Your Town
1. Introduce this activity using the sections on names of towns in Chapter 2 of the text.
Extensions
1. As a warmup, list actual Gold Country

names. Discuss what the names seem to be about (i.e., a physical feature, the people who founded the camp, an event, etc.). This will give the class a basis to work from.
2. Discuss how your town or your school got their name. Research local street names to learn about local history. Have students pick a real Gold Rush town and research and write about how it got its name (use Gold Rush

books, write to Chambers of Commerce, etc.). The origins of many names throughout the state may be found in the different books available on California place names. (How did *California* get its name, anyway?)

Directions for Make Laws for Your Town

1. Discuss Gold Rush conditions—the lack of police and jails, how miners got together and passed their own laws, etc.—before this portion of the activity. The introduction and Gold Nugget for Miners' Court (pg. 32) provide information in addition to the text.

Extensions

1. Discuss justice then and now—the similarities and the differences. Brainstorm a list of current crimes and compare it with a list of crimes that may have taken place during the Gold Rush. What crimes hardly exist anymore? What modern crimes didn't exist during the Gold Rush? What crimes do people think are more or less serious today? What are the purposes of punishment and possible punishments for different crimes?

2. Have students write a letter to a local, state, or national official about some problem of crime or punishment, and what they think should be done about it.

Directions for Decorate Your Town

1. After brainstorming, break the class into groups and have them make different signs.

Buying and Selling, Gold Rush Style (pp. 25-28)

Overview: Explore supply and demand by re-creating a Gold Rush "Merchants and Miners" scenario. Merchants decide on what to stock their store with and how to price their items. Miners shop for items to fill their basic needs for a week as a new prospector.

Materials: Sign-making material for Merchants

Directions

1. Follow the directions under Preparation.
2. Run the activity in three sessions: (1) Getting Ready to Play; (2) During Play; (3) After Play. Make each session a class period. (During Play needs an extended period.)

Preparation

1. Divide your class into Merchants and Miners. Have a minimum of three stores (a team of two Merchants each). The Miners operate independently. A good ratio is one store for every four Miners. (A class of 24 students equals 16 Miners and 4 stores.)
2. Copy two pages of Miner Bucks (pg. 28) for each Miner. This is their allotment of $50. The Merchants begin with $225 of "Funny Money" (they do not get any Miner Bucks).
3. Copy as many item card sheets (pg. 27) as there are Miners. Cut out the cards. (Consider laminating them.) Fill Merchants' orders from these cards. (NOTE: Copying one item card sheet per Miner creates a "scarcity" of

---

GOLD NUGGETS

NOTE: Use this information to supplement your After Play discussion.
- Sam Brannan helped to start the Gold Rush by spreading the news about the discovery of gold near Sutter's Mill. He was hoping to attract customers to his store. Brannan became California's first millionaire—and the first one to go broke!
- Early in the Gold Rush Sam Brannan bought all of the available gold pans in San Francisco for 20¢ and later sold them for between $8 and $16 dollars in gold. His store at Sutter's Fort made a whopping $36,000 in the first four months of the Gold Rush!
- Supplies worth $300 in July of 1848 cost $1,000 by October. By December, a breakfast of cheese, beer, sardines, and bread at Sutter's Mill cost $43. At times during the Gold Rush a single egg cost $3, and a blanket cost $60.

---

goods, so that the first Merchants to order may get a majority of one item before you sell out. If you want an "infinite" market for Merchants, copy more item cards.)
4. Copy one Merchant sheet for each Merchant team and one Miner sheet for each Miner. (pp. 25-26)

Session 1: Getting Ready to Play

Explain the game to your students. Give them their respective sheets. Explain that some of the items on the list are "necessities" and some are "extras." They should try and figure out which are which before they decide on what to order and what to buy.

The Miners receive more points for the necessities they buy than for the extras. They should try to buy items to cover all of their needs (i.e., some food, some tools, etc.). Merchants should try to stock their stores based on what they think Miners will buy.

Merchant teams . . .

1. Fill out their order form. *They should not confer with other Merchant teams or any Miner.*
2. Check their math, and give their sheet to you. You double-check their math, and then return their order form/instruction sheet and give them one item card for each item they bought (5 picks=5 pick cards). Fill orders on a first-come, first-served basis. If an item is sold out, the Merchants need to select a different one and re-figure their math.
3. Make large signs for their store, advertising available items and the prices they choose to charge for them (in whole dollar amounts).

Miners . . .

1. Use the supply list to write a paragraph

---

about what they want to buy and why. Stress that they should carefully prioritize the items they want to buy (they only have $50). Use their written work during the discussion in Session 3.
2. Can cut out and color their money while the Merchants are making their signs.

Session 2: During Play

NOTE: Allow enough time in this session to let the dynamics of supply and demand take place (i.e., Merchants sensing what is popular and what isn't and raising and lowering prices accordingly, bargaining, etc.). Students will also need time to compute Merchant profit and Miner scores.

1. Miners shop around at the different stores. When they buy an item, they give the Merchant the correct amount of money and the Merchant gives them the proper item card. After Merchants have sold out of an item, they should cross it off their sign.
2. Encourage bargaining, sales, raising and lowering prices as the market will bear, and so on. (It might occur to one or more of the Miners to get something they need from another Miner through sale or trade, or even to buy goods at a cheap price to re-sell to other Miners.)
3. When the game is over (either the Miners have each spent all of their money, or the period is over), the Merchants should figure out their profit while you lead the Miners through determining their score (see below).

Determining Miners' Scores

1. Miners put a check on their shopping list next to each item they bought.
2. Walk them through the scoring based on the following values:

Necessities

Items 1-3 (Tools): If they bought one of these three items, 10 points; two out of three, 15 points; all three, 20 points. Use the same scoring system for items 7-9 (Food), 13-15 (Utilities), and 19-21 (Shelter).

Extras

Items 4-6, 10-12, 16-18: Score 4 points for each item selected.

Bonus Points

If Miners have at least one item from each of 1-3, 7-9, 13-15, and 19-21, they have covered all of their basic needs and receive a 25-point bonus. (NOTE: A space has been left on the Miner sheet to help you with this. Tell Miners, "If you have item 1, 2, *or* 3, put a check next to the A on your sheet. If you have item 7, 8, *or* 9, put a check next to the B." Continue through 13-15 and 19-21. Then say, "If you have a check next to all four letters, give yourself 25 points.")

Session 3: After Play

1. Lead a discussion focusing on what happened during play. Examples of questions to ask:
- "First everyone shopped at John and Billy's store. Why?" [They were the cheapest.]

- "Joe and Lisa sold everything in their store, but only made $25. Why?" [Their items were too cheap.]
- "What if Merchants agreed not to undersell each other?" [A monopoly would be formed.]
- "How could Miners beat a monopoly?" [Form teams and pool their resources.]
- "As a team, should you share a gold pan?" [No, each would want to pan.] "A frying pan?" [Yes, cook meals together.]

2. Have Miners use their written paragraphs to briefly explain why they sought the items they did. Have Merchants state their profit and explain why they stocked their stores as they did. Don't focus on the wisdom of the choices made; the purpose of this is to show the class what drives prices (i.e., if there are only a few of an item that is in demand, it is priced high, and vice-versa). For example, if all the Merchants but one stocked picks and no gold pans, but all the Miners wanted gold pans, the Merchant with gold pans could demand a high price. In this example, it would be interesting for the class to see *why* most of the Merchants thought picks would be in demand, and *why* the Miners wanted gold pans instead.

3. Follow up with a general discussion of supply and demand. (What drives the price of goods? How does this affect what we buy today? How does scarcity affect value?)

Teacher Thought Points

1. If the role of the Miner seems too difficult for students, let them: (1) pair up; (2) decide on their different duties within a gold mining team; (3) shop together (pooling their money and bargaining skills).

2. Consider discussing Merchant profits. If a Merchant team made $50, could they expect to do well in the gold fields?

Panning for Gold (pg. 29)

Overview: Students learn the basics of panning for gold in a hands-on exercise.

Materials: Large round tub or bucket per group (or station); mixture of sand, water, and BBs; "gold pans" for students who can't bring any; one small shovel per group

Directions

1. Discuss the kinds of containers that make good gold pans.

2. Put the sand, water, and BBs, into the tubs. For realism, spray paint the BBs gold. If you use gravel in your mixture, be sure the BBs are the heaviest item in the mix in order to simulate the weight of gold.

3. Review the directions. Break the class into groups of 3 or 4 per tub or turn at the station.

Extensions

1. Use "Things to Think About" as a springboard to talk about gravity, density, forces acting on circular motion, and the scientific processes used to test gold.

2. Come up with a gold-testing experiment that utilizes the basics of the scientific method (formulate a hypothesis, test the hypothesis, observe and analyze the results).

Music to a Miner's Ears (pg. 30)

(Create a Miner's Song / Make a Homemade Instrument)

Overview: Students rewrite favorite songs as the miners did and make musical instruments to form a miners' band.

Materials: See instruments/components list on student page

Directions for Create a Miner's Song

1. Allow students to form groups and rewrite a favorite song with Gold Rush words.

2. Have students rehearse their songs and then perform them a capella or accompanied by the instruments they make in the Make a Homemade Instrument section.

Extension

1. Record groups on audio/video tape.

Directions for Make a Homemade Instrument

1. Don't be limited by the suggestions listed; be creative in the materials you bring in and the instruments made.

Tell Me a Wild One (pg. 31)

Overview: Students write endings and morals for a story about a Gold Rush town's name.

Materials: Writing paper

Directions

1. Read the story starter aloud, with emphasis, to make it come alive.

2. Discuss the concept of a story's moral. Read a few examples from Aesop's Fables.

3. Have students read their endings and morals aloud.

Extensions

1. Have a story-telling contest with categories such as tall tales, jokes, or re-telling a story from the text (in their own words). Have the class vote by secret ballot, evaluating stories on delivery, creativity, etc.

2. Have students research how a real Gold Rush town got its name and tell the story (see Extension #2 of Start Your Own Gold Rush Town: Name Your Town).

Miners' Court (pp. 32-33)

Overview: Students explore Gold Country justice in a "Miners' Court" mock trial.

Suggestions

1. Perform Readers' Theatre (pp. 51-61) as a warmup to this activity.

Directions

1. Pick six actors for the roles described on the information slips page (pg. 33). The judge's role is very hard. A slip is included

for whoever plays this role, *but for your first mock trial you may want to act as the judge.*

2. Copy page 32 for each student. Copy page 33 and cut out the slips. Give the slip for a specific role to the student with that role.

3. Review the slips/roles individually with each main actor. *Stress they are not to share their information slip with anyone.*

4. Draw the crime scene sketch on the chalkboard. Set up the classroom so the judge is in a dominant position. Have the witnesses in one place, and miners Sam and Jake separated from miner Matt.

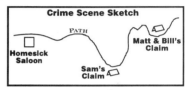

5. Guide the judge throughout the trial. Make sure all of the main actors get to speak. A good flow for the trial follows:
- Introduction/case summation by the judge
- Matt accuses Sam and says why
- Sam tells his story
- Judge calls witnesses one at a time to tell what they saw
- Miners Matt and Sam (and friend Jake) raise their hands and the judge calls on them to question each other and the witnesses
- Judge has jury vote as directed on Judge's information slip

After the Trial: Follow-up Discussions

1. Have the actors read their information slips to the class. What are the class' feelings after hearing what really happened? Why are rules of behavior in court or ideas like "innocent until proven guilty" important? What happens when trials are held without clear rules or standards of evidence? Could emotions lead people to punish an innocent party? Have the students ever been punished for something they didn't do?

2. How do we feel about someone who has been accused of doing something wrong? Does the accusation change our feelings toward the person? What if the accusation turns out to be false?

3. In America, people accused of crimes have many rights that protect them. For instance, sometimes accused people go free because the police broke rules in gathering evidence. Which would be better—a system of justice that makes it easier to convict an accused party (even if some innocent people get punished, too), or one that makes it harder to prove guilt (even if some guilty people get away with their crimes)?

Points to Keep in Mind

1. If a student is the judge, help him or her. The trial situation is very dynamic, with many possibilities. For example, if the actors start to imply Matt actually *planted* the gold on Sam's claim, the judge might suggest in

an angry voice that the real scoundrel is Matt, and maybe he should be tried instead.

2. This exercise simulates a freewheeling Miners' Court, with little of the formal structure of a modern trial. It could be a rowdy affair filled with angry miners, cat calls, interruptions, and arguing. Emotions and personal likes and dislikes probably decided many of the outcomes. The presumption of innocence and the standard of proof of guilt beyond a reasonable doubt were not as strict back then. Be flexible and encourage "living the roles" (just be prepared to bring the trial back on course or help out if it stalls). Use these comparisons of courts then and now as a follow-up discussion point (along with other discussions suggested in After the Trial: Follow-up Discussions).

Extension

1. Take a Gold Rush era crime (the text has numerous accounts of bandits and badmen) and write a mock trial script for your class.

Wanted! (pg. 34)

Overview: Students research Gold Rush era outlaws and make a Wanted poster of them.
Materials: Art supplies for making posters
Directions

1. The text contains numerous accounts of Gold Rush outlaws that students can use.
2. Give sample phrases like "Wanted for Murder" or "armed and dangerous" or "Wanted Dead or Alive" or "Also known as . . . ." Students who have not seen Westerns or wanted posters may not be familiar with the terminology, or concepts like aliases.
3. Stress attention to detail (e.g., Yankee Jim had a Yankee "accent," Joaquin Murrieta spoke Spanish).

Shut the Box (pp. 35-36)

Overview: A dice game in honor of the 49ers. Students design their own "Gold Rush" game board.
Materials: One pair of six-sided dice and nine markers (beans, etc.) per group; paper to keep score on; a game board per group (For making game boards: cardboard, glue, art supplies for coloring)
Directions

1. Make one copy of pages 35 and 36 for each student. Review the directions, and then break students into groups of 3-6 players.
2. Have each students make their own game board (see page 36).
3. To play as a betting game, each player contributes a certain amount of "gold" (beans, small rocks sprayed gold, etc.) to the "kitty" at the start of a game. The winner collects all the "gold" in the kitty!

49er (pp. 37-38)

Overview: A math-based card game named in the 49ers' honor. Students can make their own "Gold Rush" deck of cards.
Materials: A deck of cards (Jokers optional) per group, paper to keep score on
Directions

1. Copy pages 37 and 38 back to back for each student. Review the directions, and then break students into groups of 2-5 players.
2. To play as a betting game, each player contributes a certain amount of "gold" (beans, small rocks sprayed gold, etc.) to the "kitty" at the start of a game. The winner collects all the "gold" in the kitty!

Extension

1. Have students make a "Gold Rush" deck of cards (see page 38).

Get the News Out! (pp. 39-40)
(Edit This Newspaper / Publish Your Town Newspaper)

Overview: A two-part activity. Students first edit a Gold Rush newspaper for grammar, spelling, and factual errors and then break into groups to publish their own Gold Rush newspapers. Activities can be done separately. Compile many of your class's experiences and activities in writing. An excellent way to culminate your Gold Rush study.
Materials: Edit This Newspaper (none); Publish Your Town Newspaper (paper for newspaper, glue for paste-up, pens/paints/crayons for illustrations)
Directions for Edit This Newspaper

1. Activity can be done in teams. Consider doing this on Day 1 (see #3, Directions (General) for Publish Your Town Newspaper).
Directions (General) for Publish Your Town Newspaper

1. Decide on paper size and number of pages per newspaper. Use 11 x 17-inch sheets or butcher paper for more exciting papers.
2. Decide how students will generate article and illustration topics. If you wait until the end of your Gold Rush study, then students can base their articles on the activities. (Who panned the most gold, what name and laws did the town get, what happened in the Miners' Court, etc.) Otherwise, students can research Gold Rush era stories and events (both in the Gold Country and elsewhere) and write about them.
3. Decide on a newspaper schedule. Here is a sample one-week schedule. Day 1: General discussion and Edit This Newspaper activity. Day 2: Groups pick newspaper name and discuss and assign roles/stories/other jobs. Days 3 and 4: Writers, illustrators, and ad people create stories and drawings; Editor makes the grid, checks to make sure stuff will

fit, and writes fill material. Day 5: Groups re-convene to proofread one another's stories and place the corrected articles, ads, etc., onto the grid.
Directions (Specific) for Publish Your Town Newspaper

1. As a class compare different newspapers (a local paper, a major paper like USA Today, etc.). Compare the following elements:
- masthead
- headlines
- illustrations and captions
- columns (#, size, how many per story, etc.)
- front page stories
- advertisements (space they take up)
2. When comparing papers ask questions such as: Which looks the most interesting? Why? How does each paper bring attention to important articles? What do they consider to be important stories and sections? Why is so much space devoted to ads?
3. Discuss a newspaper grid. Put a sample grid on the chalkboard (one is given below). Grids will vary depending on the paper size.

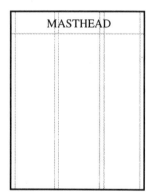

4. Divide class into groups. We recommend 6-9 students producing a four-page paper.
5. Assign roles within each group. For a 6 to 9-member group we recommend 1 editor in chief, 3-4 reporters, 1-2 illustrators, and 1-2 ad people. (If you did Buying and Selling, Gold Rush Style, then the Merchants could make ads for their stores.) Assign your best writers as reporters, your best drawers as illustrators, etc., or have the members of each group draw roles from a hat.
6. Review each role with your class. (One role of an illustrator could be to design a masthead.) Explain how you want students to come up with their articles (e.g., based on their activities, based on historical events, or a combination of the two).
7. Explain the schedule (what you expect accomplished each day). Monitor groups as they work, offering suggestions when needed.
Extensions

1. Include a Classified Section in your papers where students can create individual ads.
2. Discuss the importance of the newspaper then as compared to now where there are many other means of communication (e.g., radio, television, computer).

START YOUR OWN GOLD RUSH TOWN

Welcome to California! You and your fellow prospectors have gathered from all over the world in hopes of striking it rich in the gold fields. With so many fortune seekers arriving every day, it's time to start your own Gold Rush town. You'll need to give your town a name, make some town laws, and decorate your new home.

Name Your Town

Many towns and mining camps in California's Gold Country had colorful names. There were places called Sorefinger, Flea Valley, Poverty Flat, and even Skunk Gulch. It's a lot of fun to guess how the miners came up with these names. Many times the real story is stranger than anything you could make up!

Directions

1. As a class, brainstorm a list of possible names for your new town. Each person who suggests a name should tell a story that explains the name, or give a reason why the name would be a good one for your town. For instance, the name could be based on a tall tale that you make up, on your school's name, or on something special about your class, school, or community.

2. Discuss the list of names, and have a vote to decide which name the class likes the best.

Make Laws for Your Town

Your new town needs laws to encourage everyone to behave properly. For every law, there needs to be a punishment if the law is broken. (With luck, the threat of punishment will keep people from breaking the law in the first place.) It's up to you and the other townspeople (your classmates) to come up with the "crimes" you want to prevent, and the punishments for lawbreakers.

Directions

1. As a class, brainstorm a list of crimes that might have been committed in Gold Rush days, like horse stealing and claim jumping (stealing another miner's claim).

2. Discuss which crimes are more serious than others, and why. For instance, robbing a miner of his gold is probably more serious than taking a can of beans, but less serious than stealing a horse.

   You might want to sort your list of crimes into two categories, just as lawmakers do today. *Misdemeanors* are minor offenses, such as disrupting the peace. *Felonies* are serious offenses, such as armed robbery and murder.

3. Brainstorm and debate appropriate Gold Rush punishments for each crime on your list. The punishments for misdemeanors are fairly light (often the offender simply pays a fine), while the punishments for felonies can be very severe (going to jail, or worse!). Some of the punishments the

miners came up with were tongue lashing (scolding), whipping, branding, banishment, and hanging. As a "town," vote on the best punishment for each crime.

4. Now repeat steps 1 through 3 for "crimes" that could disrupt your classroom Gold Rush activities, such as speaking out of turn, being disrespectful to a classmate, or failing to do your part in a group activity. Be sure to talk about why some behaviors are more serious "crimes" than others. Try to come up with punishments that are fair and appropriate for your class.

Things to Think About

1. Why was stealing a horse a severe crime?

2. Why was banishment a very bad punishment?

3. The 49ers didn't have jails or people to watch them. What kind of punishments can you come up with that don't require a jail?

4. Why might someone commit a crime even when they know it is against the law?

Decorate Your Town

No town is complete without signs. Now that you have a town name and laws, design and make signs, posters, and banners to decorate your town.

Directions

1. As a class, brainstorm different kinds of signs to post in the town. Here are some possible types:

◇ A sign showing your town's name and population (the number of people in your class). If you want to get really fancy, find out your community's elevation and include it on the sign.

◇ Posters showing the town's laws and the punishments for breaking them. (Should these be fancy and decorative scrolls, or simple, bold signs with a BIG warning?)

◇ A banner welcoming newcomers to the town.

◇ Signs showing the distances to other locations in California, such as Sutter's Fort (Sacramento) and San Francisco. (Use a state map to measure the distances from your community.)

2. Design and make your signs, and post them around the town (classroom).

BUYING AND SELLING, GOLD RUSH STYLE: Merchant Sheet

You are enterprising young prospectors who have realized that few strike it rich searching for gold, but that a fortune can be made supplying those who chase it. You pool your life savings and come up with $225 to outfit your new store in the Gold Country. Your goal is to make as much money as you can by selling the items you purchase for your store.

Getting Ready to Play

1. Decide together which items you want to stock in your store. Write the quantity of each item you want to order in the column labeled "Quantity Ordered." The list includes both necessities and "extras." The Miners will be trying to buy necessities to satisfy their basic needs for a week in the gold fields. Try to anticipate what their necessities might be. You do not have to buy one of everything. (NOTE: *You may not talk to other Merchants or to Miners.*)

2. As you decide on items, multiply the quantity of the item you want by the Item Price. Put the answer in the "Total Cost" column. For example, if you buy 5 picks at $3 each, write $15 under "Total Cost" across from Picks. You would then have $210 left to spend ($225-$15=$210). Keep careful track of your money—you can't spend more than you have.

3. Complete your order and check your math. Give your order to your supplier (teacher). Your supplier will give you one item card for each item you buy. If an item is sold out, order a different item and re-figure your math.

4. Decide on the prices to charge for each item. Use only whole dollar amounts in your prices. Look at the hints below for help in pricing. Make a large sign advertising your store. List the items you have to sell along with the prices.

During Play

1. Miners will come to your store to buy supplies. If there is a huge demand for an item, consider raising your price for that item. If an item isn't selling, consider lowering the price. Miners may try to bargain for lower prices. It's up to you to decide whether or not to lower the price of an item in order to make a sale.

2. Collect the exact amount in "Miner Bucks" for each item you sell, and give the Miner the right item card.

3. When you have no item cards left for an item, you are sold out. Cross the item off your sign.

After Play

1. Figure out how much money you have made (your profit). First, add up the value (the amount you spent) for all the item cards you didn't sell. Add to this total the "Miner Bucks" you collected. Then add any money you didn't spend from your original $225. This sum is the total of all your money plus the value of your unsold goods. Subtract $225 (the total you started with). The result is your profit.

ORDER FORM Item	Item Price	Quantity Ordered	Total Cost
1. Shovel	$4		
2. Pick	$3		
3. Gold pan	$2		
4. Book	$2		
5. 6 eggs	$5		
6. 1 pound tobacco	$2		
7. 5 pounds beans	$2		
8. Sack of potatoes	$3		
9. 3 pounds jerky	$3		
10. Deck of cards	$1		
11. Shirt	$4		
12. Pocket watch	$6		
13. Lantern & fuel	$5		
14. Rifle & ammunition	$12		
15. Fire starting tools	$1		
16. Dice	$1		
17. Hard candy	$1		
18. Pillow	$3		
19. Blanket	$8		
20. Tent	$13		
21. Canvas tarp	$10		
TOTAL SPENT			

Hints

1. Set your prices higher than what you paid for each item—otherwise, you won't make any money!

2. Although you want to make the most profit you can, remember that the Miners don't have a lot of money. Sometimes it might be better to charge a lower price and sell more items than you would at a higher price.

3. Don't sell your items too cheap just to get rid of them—the two of you have to live off of your profits!

BUYING AND SELLING, GOLD RUSH STYLE: Miner Sheet

You have chosen to chase the golden dream and try to strike it rich. You have arrived in the gold fields with the clothes on your back, some eating and cooking utensils, and $50 left from your tough westward journey. Now you need a week's worth of supplies so you can begin your hunt for gold. Your goal is to buy the most supplies you can for your money, making sure you have supplies to cover all of your needs.

Getting Ready to Play

1. Look over the list of supplies. Write a paragraph or two about which supplies you will try to buy first and why. Some of the items on your list are necessities and some are extras. Decide which items you will want to buy in order to take care of all your basic needs (food, tools, and so on).

2. When it's time to play the game, your teacher will then give you $50 in "Miner Bucks."

During Play

1. Shop around at the different stores. Buy the items you need at the best price you can. Pay the Merchants the exact amount in Miner Bucks for each purchase. Make sure you get an item card for each item you buy.

2. Try to take care of necessities first. Remember, you will have to go out into the cold mountains with only the items you buy today and the clothes and utensils you started with.

After Play

1. For each item card you received, put a check on your shopping list next to that item.

2. Your teacher will then show you how to score your purchases.

Hints

1. Don't be afraid to bargain with the merchants to get a lower price. The Merchants know that they can't make any money if no one buys their goods.

2. Shop around, but don't spend too long—you might discover that something you need has sold out!

3. If the Merchants don't have what you want, or if the price is too high, try to get another item that will take care of the same basic need.

SUPPLIES LIST

1. Shovel
2. Pick
3. Gold pan
4. Book
5. 6 eggs
6. 1 pound tobacco
7. 5 pounds beans
8. Sack of potatoes
9. 3 pounds jerky
10. Deck of cards
11. Shirt
12. Pocket watch
13. Lantern & fuel
14. Rifle & ammunition
15. Fire starting tools
16. Dice
17. Hard candy
18. Pillow
19. Blanket
20. Tent
21. Canvas tarp

Use this box for scoring purposes only:

A: _____ B: _____ C: _____ D: _____

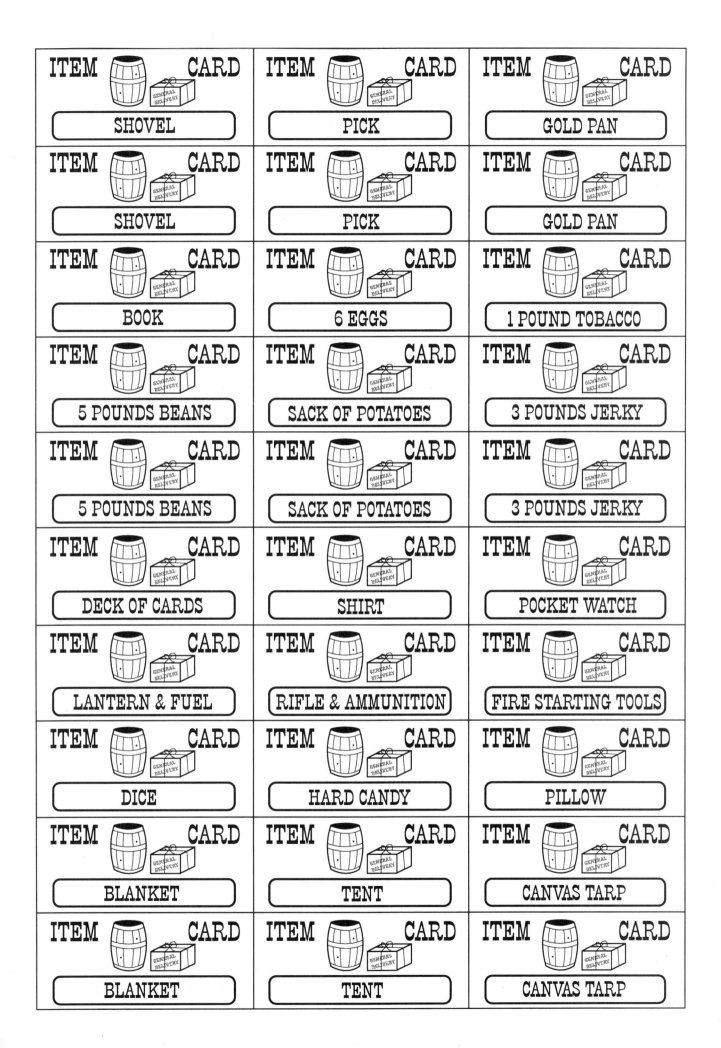

ITEM CARD	ITEM CARD	ITEM CARD
SHOVEL	PICK	GOLD PAN
SHOVEL	PICK	GOLD PAN
BOOK	6 EGGS	1 POUND TOBACCO
5 POUNDS BEANS	SACK OF POTATOES	3 POUNDS JERKY
5 POUNDS BEANS	SACK OF POTATOES	3 POUNDS JERKY
DECK OF CARDS	SHIRT	POCKET WATCH
LANTERN & FUEL	RIFLE & AMMUNITION	FIRE STARTING TOOLS
DICE	HARD CANDY	PILLOW
BLANKET	TENT	CANVAS TARP
BLANKET	TENT	CANVAS TARP

PANNING FOR GOLD

Wow! You're finally in California! A clear, cold stream is pouring out of the Sierra Nevada, just waiting for you to find its riches. Your brand-new gold mining pan is in your hands and the excitement of gold fever races through your body. It's time to put on your prospector's cap and dig in to these golden rules of panning.

Golden Rules of Panning

1. Begin by choosing a good "gold pan." Early gold seekers used many different containers as "gold pans." Some miners even used their frying pans! Try to find a shallow container. The best containers have a smooth bottom, a corner along the bottom where gold can collect, and ridges along the sides. Bring one or two containers from home that you think will help you trap and keep all your gold on the bottom. Be creative!

2. Use a shovel and dig deep into the sand and gravel. Empty the shovel contents into your pan. Hold the pan completely under water and shake it strongly side to side. Use your palm to hit the side of your pan a few times. Since gold is heavier than sand, it will settle to the bottom while the lighter material floats away.

3. Keeping your pan under water, continue to shake it from side to side. *Be careful not to swirl your pan too forcefully,* or all your gold may be swept away. Use your hands to stir up the contents of your pan, breaking up any lumps. Pick out any large rocks, but check them for gold first.

4. Slightly tilt the pan away from you so that the side of the pan closer to you is just out of the water. As you continue to shake the pan, use your thumb or the back of your hand and push out the sand and gravel that collects at the edge. As the pan empties, remember to keep shaking it from side to side so the gold settles to the bottom. Soon you should be able to see your gold!

Gold panning is hard work, but if you keep practicing, you'll be grinning from ear to ear when you finally glimpse that gold in the bottom of your pan!

Things to Think About

1. Why do you think the "ridges" in a gold pan are important?

2. What kinds of containers would not be good to use for panning?

3. Why does shaking your pan help gold settle to the bottom of the pan, while swirling it causes the gold to be pushed out toward the edges?

4. If you found gold in a large rock, how would you separate the different elements from each other?

HOW TO TEST FOR GOLD

If you ever pan in a real river and you see something glittering at the bottom of your pan, you will want to be sure that it is gold and not *pyrite,* or fool's gold. Fool's gold looks like real gold, but is actually iron and sulfur. Miners had several ways to verify gold:

◆ Testing the "gold's" density with an equal weight under water.

◆ Dipping the material in nitric acid. If the material dissolved, it was not gold.

◆ Heating the "gold" and seeing if it smoked or smelled like sulfur.

Though these methods left little room for doubt, you can use a simpler, old Gold Rush test to quickly find out whether your gold is real. Gold is a very soft metal. If you hit it with a hammer, it will only flatten. If you have fool's gold, your "gold" will shatter into pieces.

MUSIC TO A MINER'S EARS

Create a Miner's Song

At the end of a hard day's work, weary miners needed some entertainment. One way they passed the time was by making music and having sing-alongs. In order to create songs that expressed their feelings, sometimes the miners took popular melodies like "O, Susannah!" and wrote new words to them. (See the example in the box.) Try writing some Gold Rush songs the way the miners did. Then stage your own sing-along!

Directions

Imagine that you're on your way to the gold fields, or that you're already living in a small mining camp. Choose a favorite song that most of your classmates know, and make up your own words to describe your feelings and experiences in the Gold Rush. Teach your new song to your classmates so they can sing along.

Make a Homemade Instrument

Making music was one of the miners' favorite pastimes. Some of them had brought musical instruments with them to the gold fields. Others made up their own instruments, or kept time to the music using whatever "music makers" they had handy.

Directions

Give your mining camp its own Gold Rush band by making musical instruments out of everyday objects. Pick an instrument to create from the list below, or design your own. (Why aren't electric guitars a good choice?) Experiment with different combinations of materials and listen for variations in sound. When you have completed your instrument, you may want to decorate it.

SUNG TO "O, SUSANNAH!"

*And all of us—have we not left
Our best of life for this?
But cheer we up! we will return
Laden with gold and bliss!
Then saddle our mules! away we go
With hopes by fancy led,
To where the Sacramento flows
Over its glittering bed!*

*CHORUS:
Oh California!
Thou land of glittering dreams,
Where the yellow dust and diamonds, boys,
Are found in all thy streams!*

Footnote: From J. S. Holliday, *The World Rushed In: The California Gold Rush Experience.*

◇ **Banjo:** Cut a hole in a milk carton or shoe box. Stretch different-sized rubber bands over the hole.

◇ **Bells:** Fill glasses with varying amounts of water and *gently* strike with a metal spoon.

◇ **Cymbals:** Strike different-sized metal pot lids together or hit them with a metal spoon.

◇ **Drum:** Use an empty oatmeal box and bang the lid with a wooden spoon.

◇ **Maracas:** Fill a small paper bag with rice or popcorn kernels until the bottom is just covered.

◇ **Washboard:** Glue two long, thin pieces of wood to one large block of wood. Place them no farther apart than the length of a popsicle stick. You may want them closer together on one end than the other. Now glue popsicle sticks across the two thin pieces of wood, about ½ inch apart. (See picture.) Experiment by scraping across the popsicle sticks with different objects (try the flat side and the edge of another popsicle stick for starters).

◇ **Wood blocks:** Use glue to cover one side of the wood blocks with sandpaper. Rub the sandpaper sides together; you may also strike the blocks together.

Hands-On History: Tales & Treasures of the California Gold Rush — Copyright 1995 • Ghost Town Publications • Carmel, California

TELL ME A WILD ONE

After a long day's work you and your fellow gold seekers love to hear and tell stories. Jokes, tall tales, and true accounts are welcome breaks from your life of toil and sweat.

One night you are sitting around a campfire with a bunch of other miners from nearby claims. Across the fire from you a newcomer is sitting, staring into the fire and listening to the wild tales that are being told. Suddenly the new fellow looks up and your eyes meet. He hesitates and then asks, "Say, how did this place get its name, anyway?"

The miners fall silent. A few of the old-timers wink at each other and then look at you. You stare off into the stars and begin to tell the young man a tale, "Well, the name Horatio's Hollow . . ."

Directions

1. Read the story below.

2. Starting on this page, and continuing on a separate sheet of paper, complete the story you are telling the newcomer. The other miners are hoping you'll tell a really tall tale to see whether the new fellow believes it, but it's up to you to figure out how the story should end.

3. After you write your story, write a one-sentence moral to your story. A moral is a lesson that can be drawn from a story. If you wrote a funny tall tale, make-up a funny moral. If you wrote a serious story, you might want a serious moral that truly teaches a lesson.

"Well, the name Horatio's Hollow goes back to the days of the first gold strikes. One day this old miner with a long gray beard came a-strollin' over that hill over there. He was all alone except for his mule, Horatio, which was loaded up with all this fellow's stuff. He was heading to the next valley over, where there had been a big gold discovery and the claims were filling up fast. He knew he should keep moving on since he still had a couple of hours of daylight left, but the river looked real inviting and he desperately needed a bath. Well, this old-timer decided to take a bath and then bed down right here where we're sittin'. He scrubbed himself up good, made himself some beans and coffee, and then tied stubborn Horatio to that tree over there and settled in for the night.

"Sometime in the night, when the moon was high and stars filled the sky, this old fellow awoke and sat straight up. He'd heard a noise. He looked over at stubborn Horatio, and Horatio was gone! His rope hung limp from the tree where the fellow had tied him. This old fellow stood up and stomped his feet into his boots. He walked over to the spot where Horatio had been tied and stood there and stared. He couldn't tell if the rope had been chewed through, or cut, but in the moonlight he could see the tracks of a mule heading away. Well, this old-timer got his gun, and moving quietly in case there were bandits nearby, he followed the tracks into the woods . . ."

_____

_____

(continued)

MINERS' COURT

Gold Country justice was not always like modern justice. Many criminals never received trials as we know them today. Especially in the early days of the Gold Rush, a group of miners might gather to decide the fate of a suspected criminal. A judge was picked from the crowd, and the juries ranged from a few miners to all of the people present. As the camps became more settled, the courts became more like courts today.

In the early days of the Gold Rush, trials often were held in cabins or other buildings. Without jails to hold prisoners, trials were held immediately and punishments were carried out swiftly. Punishments ranged from tongue lashings (scoldings) to whippings, brandings, banishment from camp, or execution. Although their system may seem cruel, the miners felt it was the only way to protect themselves against robbery and violence. Many of them were very kind, and would even take up a collection to help a man who had been banished.

Directions

1. In this activity you will conduct an early Gold Rush trial. Your teacher will assign you parts to play. Main actors include the accuser, the defendant, the judge, witnesses, and a friend of the defendant. If you are *not* picked for one of these roles, you will be a miner on the jury. Listen carefully to what is said, and remember that a miner's fate is in your hands!

2. If you are a main actor, study the information slip you are given. It will tell you what you need to know to act out your role. When you are asked questions, make up any facts you need to fill in missing information. *Do not let anyone else see your information slip!*

Setting the Stage

Miner Matt McCuldy claims that a pouch of gold was missing from his tent this morning. The pouch was found by Burly Bill, a miner who shares a claim with Matt. He found the pouch only an hour ago on miner Sappy Sam's claim. The pouch was sticking out from under a bush near the path that goes past the claim.

Many people saw miners Matt and Sam arguing last night in the large tent that serves as the Homesick Saloon. After the argument, Sam stormed out of the tent.

A few minutes ago, a group of angry miners grabbed Sam out of his tent, where he was still sleeping. The whole camp has gathered to hear the case against Sam and decide if he should be hung for stealing. You have picked a judge, fellow miner George Justice, and three witnesses have come forward. Matt wants to see Sam hung. Sam is having his friend, miner Jake, help him during his trial.

GOLD NUGGET

This is one account of an actual "Miners' Court." While other versions of this tale are slightly different, they all demonstrate the swiftness of both trials and punishments in the Gold Country . . .

The first known miners' court was held in January, 1849, in Old Dry Diggings. Five men were accused of attempted robbery. A judge and a jury of 12 miners were quickly picked. The five men were found guilty, and each was sentenced to 39 lashes with a rope.

Right after the lashings, three of the five men were recognized by someone as being wanted for a crime involving murder a few months earlier in Stanislaus. Those three, barely conscious from the lashings and unable to speak or stand, were immediately put on trial again. This time all of the miners acted as the jury. When the judge asked them what should be done, the 200 miners shouted "Hang them!"

Information Slips—Cut out and give to each main actor.

Witness One, miner Rex Runout: When they were arguing about something in the saloon last night, you heard Sam tell Matt that he would get even with him. Matt laughed and said something you couldn't hear.

Witness Two, card dealer Freddy Fast Finger: You work in the Homesick Saloon. You heard Sam accuse Matt of cheating in cards. They got into an argument. Sam said something you couldn't hear, and you heard Matt laugh and say, "That's what you think!" You saw Matt with his pouch after Sam had stormed out of the tent. The pouch looked very full. After Sam stormed out, Matt stayed for an hour and played cards and drank.

Witness Three, miner Burly Bill: During the night you heard your partner, miner Matt, come home and crawl into his tent. This morning he woke you up shouting that his gold was missing and that the "scoundrel miner Sam" had stolen it and should be hung. It was Sunday, so you walked into town for a church service. When you passed Sam's claim, you saw his feet sticking out of his tent and heard him snoring. Suspicious because of what Matt had said, you looked around and saw your partner's pouch sticking out from under a bush near Sam's tent. The pouch was almost empty.

Defendant, miner Sappy Sam: You got into an argument with miner Matt last night at the saloon after you accused him of cheating in a card game you two played in together (you saw him pull a card out of his sleeve). Matt won 5 ounces of gold from you in that game. In anger you told him you would get even. He laughed and said, "That's what you think!" You stormed out of the saloon and met your friend miner Jake, who walked to your tent with you. After he left, you went to sleep. You woke up this morning when a bunch of angry miners dragged you out of your tent and carried you to the trial. They said you stole Matt's pouch from his tent after you left the saloon. You asked Jake to sit with you during the trial and help you, and he agreed. Together plan what questions you will ask. Why did Matt accuse you anyway . . . , might he be framing you? Where did Matt put the pouch when he went to sleep if you are supposed to have stolen it? Did Burly Bill hear anyone other than Matt during the night? Did Matt accuse you before or after the pouch was discovered? Did Matt walk past your tent on his way home?

Miner Sam's friend, miner Jake: You have agreed to sit next to Sam during the trial and help him with questions. You saw Sam last night after he had stormed out of the saloon, and you walked with him to his tent. He told you how Matt had cheated him at cards. He seemed tired after he settled down. You left and went back to your tent. Listen closely to all that is said. The questions you ask the witnesses may keep your friend from getting a harsh punishment. Talk with Sam and together figure out what questions you will ask.

Accuser, miner Matt McCuldy: You scoundrel! You got into an argument with Sam last night at the saloon after he saw you pull a card out of your sleeve during a game you were playing with him. You won 5 ounces of gold from him in that game, but if people find out you are a card cheat you could be severely punished. Sam said he would get even with you. You laughed and told him, "That's what you think!" You stayed another hour, and then on your way home you walked on the path past Sam's claim. When you saw Sam asleep, you took most of your gold out of your pouch and put your pouch under a bush on Sam's claim. You knew someone would find it and that Sam would be hung as a thief! This morning you woke up your partner, miner Bill, by screaming that your gold was missing and that Sam should hang. Of course, if you admit any of this, you could be in big trouble. Your job as the accuser is to make Sam look guilty and get him hung. Then he can't ruin your reputation in the camp and maybe get you punished instead! Can you convince the jury that Sam had a motive to steal your gold? What will you do if someone accuses you of framing Sam?

Judge, miner George Justice: You have been picked by your fellow miners to be the judge for Sam's trial. You know that Gold Country justice is harsh and swift, but your job is to make sure that the trial is fair. You also know that crimes can't go unpunished, and criminals make you angry. You need to make sure that both Matt and Sam get to speak, that the three witnesses (Rex Runout, Freddy Fast Finger, and Burly Bill) get to tell their stories, and that Matt and Sam get to question the witnesses and each other. Don't let the crowd get too unruly. If unexpected things happen during the trial (maybe someone else gets accused of the crime), be prepared to follow that lead by allowing the new accuser to ask questions which could prove or disprove his guilt or innocence. If you think someone else other than Sam is guilty, you might even want to suggest it and ask questions yourself. Remember, you want to see justice done. After everyone is done questioning, have the jury vote on whether Sam is guilty or innocent by raising their hands. If they pick Sam guilty, then he will be hung. If Sam is found innocent, the jury may wish to discuss whether or not to try someone else who may have been accused of a crime during the trial. If someone else is voted guilty of a crime, then take suggestions from the jury about how they should be punished. Vote on which punishment they should get. Your teacher is there to help you, so don't be afraid to ask questions.

Hands-On History: Tales & Treasures of the California Gold Rush   Copyright 1995 • Ghost Town Publications • Carmel, California

WANTED!

Crime: _____

_____

_____

Description: _____

_____

_____

Posted By: _____
(Your Name)

Cut along this line

Directions: Make a "Wanted" poster for a Gold Country outlaw. Do some reading about a famous outlaw like Black Bart or Joaquin Murrieta, and make notes of details to use in your poster. Your poster should include a portrait and a written description of the outlaw. Include any details that would help a citizen identify the criminal. Also be sure to list the crimes the person is wanted for. You might also want to announce a reward. When you are done, cut along the dotted line.

SHUT THE BOX

"Shut the Box" is a dice game that was very popular among English sailors as long ago as the 1700s. Who knows? Maybe seafarers brought the game to California! This version is adapted in honor of the 49ers and the Gold Rush. Have fun!

What You Need: (1) One pair of six-sided dice; (2) 9 markers; (3) paper and pencil to keep score; (4) a playing board (see next page); (5) betting tokens (optional).

To Play

1. The object of the game is to shut all the boxes on the board *or* to be the last surviving player. Any number of players can play, but 3-6 is best.

2. Roll the dice to determine who will play first. Highest roll goes first (roll again if there is a tie). After the first player, play passes to the left. (Note: You may each use your own game board when it is your turn, or your group can pick one game board to share. Either way, share the markers and the dice.)

3. The first player begins the game by throwing the dice and using the scores thrown to shut the boxes on the board. On each roll, the player has these choices: (a) use the total of both dice to shut one box; (b) use the dice separately to shut two boxes; or (c) use only one of the dice to shut a single box. To "shut a box," place a marker on the appropriate box. EXAMPLES:

 The player can shut the 9 box (6+3), *or* the 6 box *and* the 3 box, *or* the 6 box, *or* the 3 box.

The player can shut the 4 box (2+2) *or* the 2 box.

The player can only shut the 5 box (there is no 10 box).

4. The same player continues rolling the dice until all the boxes are shut *or* the player gets stuck. EXAMPLES:

 If the 5, 3, and 8 boxes are all shut already, the player is stuck, and the turn ends.

SHUT THE BOX

7   8   9
4   5   6
1   2   3

 If the 6 box is already shut, the player is stuck, and the turn ends.

5. When a player gets stuck before shutting all the boxes, add up the numbers in the *open* boxes. Record the total on the paper you are using to keep score. Clear off the board and pass the markers and dice to the next player. EXAMPLE:

Suppose the only open boxes are 6, 8, and 1. The player is stuck. The player is charged with 15 points (6+8+1), and the dice are passed to the next player.

6. If you shut all the boxes without getting stuck, you've won the game! The game ends immediately even if other players are waiting for their first turn.

7. If no one shuts all the boxes, continue playing and adding up all your points after each turn. Anyone who accumulates *49 points or more* is out of the game. The others continue playing until someone shuts all the boxes *or* only one player is left with fewer than 49 points. That player wins the game—even if he or she is waiting to take a turn!

35

Make Your Own "Shut the Box" Game Board

Game boards have often been very fancy creations. Design a personal Gold Rush game board for **Shut the Box.** Put a phrase in the scroll area in each box, and illustrate the sayings with pictures. Select phrases that might have been chosen by the 49ers if they were making the board. Think about the things that mattered to them. Here are some examples:

✧ *Home Sweet Home* (with a picture of the home that the argonaut left behind—or perhaps of his tent or cabin)

✧ *Mine, All Mine!* (with a picture of gold)

✧ *O, California!* (with a picture of the Bear Flag)

✧ *Lady Luck* (with a picture of dice or cards)

✧ *Black Bart* (with a picture of the outlaw)

Color your board, cut it out, and mount it on cardboard. Then use it to play **Shut the Box!**

Hands-On History: Tales & Treasures of the California Gold Rush   Copyright 1995 ◆ Ghost Town Publications ◆ Carmel, California

49er

Card games were a favorite pastime of many 49ers. Here's an exciting card game named in their honor that's easy to play—if you use your arithmetic skills and think on your feet!

What You Need: (1) standard deck of 52 playing cards (Jokers optional); (2) paper and pencil to keep score; (3) betting tokens (optional).

To Play

1. The object of *each round* is to "score a 49er" *or* force the next player to "go bust." (These terms are explained below.) Winning a round means that you are not charged with any penalty points. The object of *the game* is to have the *fewest* penalty points when the game ends.

2. To start a round, the Dealer shuffles the deck and deals the cards one at a time (face down) until everyone has 3 cards. Put the unused cards face down in a pile. This is the Draw Pile.

3. Starting to the left of the dealer, players take turns playing one card from their hand face up on the table. As each player plays his card, its value is added to the total value of the cards played in that round (see Point Values of Cards box). Each player announces the new total as he or she plays a card. EXAMPLE:

♦ Player #1 starts the round by playing the 8 of Diamonds and saying "8."

♥ Player #2 plays the 10 of Hearts and says "10 plus 8 is 18."

♠ Player #3 plays the 5 of Spades and says "18 minus 5 is 13." (Spades are "minus" cards—see box.)

♣ Player #4 plays the King of Clubs and says "13 plus 10 is 23." (Kings count as 10—see box.)

4. Immediately after playing a card, a player draws a new card from the top of the Draw Pile. Except when scoring a 49er, players should have 3 cards in their hands at all times.

5. A "minus" card (a Spade, or a Joker following a Spade) cannot be played if it would make the total value of the cards played less than zero. If

POINT VALUES OF CARDS

✧ ACE = 1
✧ 2 through 10 = Face value of card
✧ JACK, QUEEN, KING = 10

"MINUS" CARDS: The point value of *Spades* is *subtracted* from the total value of the cards played. The 2 of Spades counts as "minus 2," the Jack of Spades as "minus 10," and so on.

A *Joker* has the value of the card that was played immediately before it. If a Joker is played right after the 3 of Hearts, it counts as 3. If it is played after the 9 of Spades, it counts as minus 9 (etc.).

As cards are played, keep them in a neat stack. That way you can add up their values if there is disagreement about the current total.

all of a player's cards would make the total less than zero, the player must skip that turn.

6. As play goes on, each player tries to make the total value of all the cards played less than or equal to 49. If a player's card makes the total exactly 49, the player "scores a 49er" and wins the round. If the lowest card in a player's hand would make the total value more than 49, the player "goes bust." When this happens, the winner of the round is the player who played the last card *before* the "busted" player. EXAMPLE:

♣ Suppose Player #2 plays a card that makes the current total equal to 48.

♠ To avoid going bust, Player #3 must play a Spade or an Ace. Playing a Spade (a "minus" card) keeps the total under 49, and play continues. Playing an Ace scores a 49er (48 + 1 = 49) and wins the round!

♥ If Player #3 has no Spades or Aces, she has no card to play that would make the total 49 or less. In this case, she "goes bust," and Player #2 wins the round.

Scoring the Round

1. The winning player's score for the round is zero. The other players each add up the values of the 3 cards in their hands. These sums are the losing players' penalty points for that round.

2. In *scoring,* the values of Spades are *added* to a player's points, not subtracted. Jokers, if used, count as zero.

3. Record the players' penalty points on the scoresheet and add them to the scores from any previous rounds. The deal then passes to the player on the Dealer's left for the next round.

Winning the Game

The game ends as soon as at least one player has 49 points or more. (Usually this happens after about 3 rounds.) The winner is the player with the lowest score! (In case of a tie, the tied players split the winnings.)

Hints on Strategy—and Questions to Think About

1. Usually you should try to get rid of high-value cards early in the round so you aren't forced to "go bust" when the total gets close to 49. Also, you don't want to get stuck with lots of points in your hand if you don't win the round.

2. It's especially dangerous to play a card that makes the total 39. Why? (Think about how many cards have each possible point value.)

3. If you can't score a 49er yourself, the next best thing is to keep the total under 39. Why?

4. If you can't keep the total under 39 *or* score a 49er, the *next* best thing is to get the total as close as possible to 49 without going over. Why?

5. After you've played 49er a few times, what other ideas about strategy can you come up with? For instance, how might it help to notice how many Aces have been played? Should you try to keep at least one Spade in your hand?

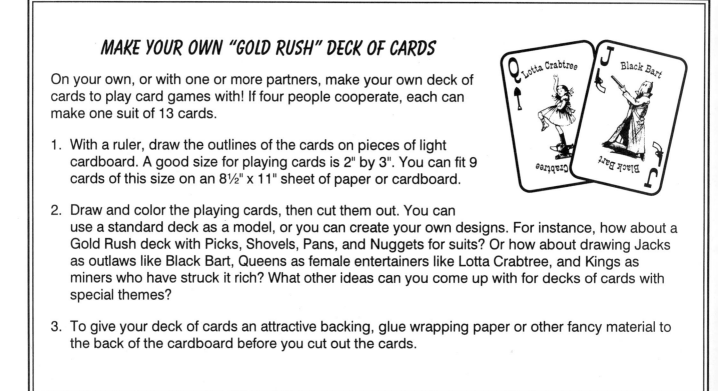

MAKE YOUR OWN "GOLD RUSH" DECK OF CARDS

On your own, or with one or more partners, make your own deck of cards to play card games with! If four people cooperate, each can make one suit of 13 cards.

1. With a ruler, draw the outlines of the cards on pieces of light cardboard. A good size for playing cards is 2" by 3". You can fit 9 cards of this size on an 8½" x 11" sheet of paper or cardboard.

2. Draw and color the playing cards, then cut them out. You can use a standard deck as a model, or you can create your own designs. For instance, how about a Gold Rush deck with Picks, Shovels, Pans, and Nuggets for suits? Or how about drawing Jacks as outlaws like Black Bart, Queens as female entertainers like Lotta Crabtree, and Kings as miners who have struck it rich? What other ideas can you come up with for decks of cards with special themes?

3. To give your deck of cards an attractive backing, glue wrapping paper or other fancy material to the back of the cardboard before you cut out the cards.

GET THE NEWS OUT!

"Read all about it, read all about it!" The latest and most exciting news is carried to the people of a town through its newspaper. Stories from around the world and around the town fill its pages. Some towns may have more than one newspaper. In this case, the newspapers compete to best provide the news that the people of the town want to read.

Edit This Newspaper

You are the editor of the Town Bugle, a Gold Country newspaper. Sadly, your reporter makes lots of mistakes. Your job is to find and correct all the mistakes in the newspaper before it's printed!

Directions

1. Write your name in the space for "Editor" on the front page of the *Bugle*. Then, carefully read the stories. Circle any mistakes you find. There are 20 mistakes in all—10 factual mistakes and 10 mistakes in language (spelling, grammar, or punctuation).

2. Fold a sheet of paper lengthwise to make two columns. Label the left column "Mistakes" and the right column "Corrections." Under "Mistakes," write down each mistake you find, along with the number of its paragraph in the *Bugle*. Under "Corrections," write the word or words that should be substituted for each mistake. Label the corrected versions to show whether you are correcting a mistake of language (L) or a mistake of fact (F). Here's an example that shows how to correct a spelling mistake in paragraph 1 of the *Bugle:*

Mistakes	Corrections
Siera (1)	Sierra (L)

HINTS

♦ You don't have to find the mistakes in order. Just keep looking until you find all 20 mistakes—or as many as you can! Every paragraph has at least one mistake.

♦ Use a dictionary to check spellings. To double-check facts, use any source that has information about the Gold Rush. Be sure to watch out for names, places, and dates.

Publish Your Town Newspaper

Does your mining town have any exciting news it's bursting to report? Now's your chance! You will be working in a group to design and publish your own Gold Rush town newspaper.

Directions

You will have one of four different roles. Here are the duties assigned to each role:

Editor in chief: Leads the discussion of what to call the paper, what stories to include, how to lay it out, etc. The editor also assigns the stories and illustrations to the reporters and illustrators, finalizes the layout grid, and writes any filler bulletins or stories.

Reporter: Gathers facts and interviews people. Then writes stories using the information collected.

Illustrator: Draws pictures to illustrate articles or special events in the paper.

Ad person: Writes advertisements for businesses and special events. What kind of stores would there be and what would they sell? What kind of special events might want to be advertised?

TOWN BUGLE

Volume I , Number 1

April 1, 1852

Writer: I.M. Careless

Editor:

RUSH FOR GOLD GOES ON!

(1) "Gold!" is still the cry in the hills and gullies of the Siera Nevada. Every day brings thousands of wild-eyed prospectors to our camps and towns. They come east across the snowy Rockies, and inland from the harbor of San Francisco. They come across the Atlantic from China and overland from St. Joseph, Missourri.

(2) In the gold fields, men from Australia work side by side with men from Chili. A babble of languages rises from the camps. At Frenchman's Creek, men from Paris curse in their native German, while men from London answer in their native English. But everyone understands the sound of one word—"gold"!

History of the Gold Rush

(3) The great Gold Rush began on January 24, 1849. On that day James Marshall made his famous discovery while he was bilding a fort on the South Fork of the American River. Before long "49ers" were swarming over the area.

Mining Techniques

(4) At first prospectors used hydraulic mining to take the gold from streams. But as gold became harder to find, panning became more populer. This method involves shooting a jet of water at a hillside. It takes more men and is more expensive, but it is surely the method of the future.

California's Future

(5) The effects of the Gold Rush will be felt far into the future. Thanks to the rush for gold, California became the nation's 21st state in 1850. At the entrance to the Golden Gate, the great city of Sacramento will rise as a permanent reminder of the rush for gold.

Prospectors flocking into San Francisco.

MAN FOUND MURDERED

(6) A grim discovery was made this week near a local minning camp, the body of Flap Jack Jenkins was found inside his cabin. According to rumor, Jenkins had recently made a large gold strike. No gold was found in the cabin.

(7) The search is on for the killer or killers. If suspects is found, a sensational trial is sure to follow. Watch the *Bugle* for details!

FLEA EPIDEMIC IN SAN FRANCISCO

(8) Travelers to San Francisco have had their fill of mosquitoes and other pests by the time they arrive (especially if they have come by way of Pamana). But there is little relief to be found in the chilly bayside town, for flea's have arrived by the thousands. While men come to California seeking gold, their tiny fellow travelers are out for blood!

THE LURE
AND LORE OF GOLD

✧ Digging for Numbers

✧ The Lucky Miner Mine

✧ Mining for Information

✧ Curly Hair Sam's Treasure

✧ As Good As Gold Crossword Puzzle

Digging for treasure! The lure and lore of gold has driven mankind for centuries. Whether searching for treasures once found and then lost, or digging deep to find that shining gold nugget, man has long been enchanted by this magical metal. Our expressions reflect its magic, and our stories are rich with the theme of gold woven through them.

This section's activities integrate the teaching of skills from across the curriculum while building on the California Gold Rush, the theme of gold, and the idea of digging for "treasures." In Digging for Numbers, students utilize basic arithmetic to "dig" for answers to complete Gold Rush-oriented word problems. They are then introduced to probability and fractions as they try to find the gold at the end of the Lucky Miner Mine. In Mining for Information, the richness of public and school libraries are discovered as students use library skills to mine for nuggets of information, and map skills are made fun while they look for Curly Hair Sam's Treasure. Finally, students come to realize how frequently "gold" can be found in our stories and expressions as they complete the As Good As Gold Crossword Puzzle.

Digging for Numbers (pg. 43)

Overview: Students use basic arithmetic to complete Gold Rush-based word problems and a chart.

The Lucky Miner Mine (pg. 44)

Overview: Students are exposed to the concept of probability and to simple fraction conversions as they work through a puzzle using clues and hints to help them.

Directions

1. This may be a difficult activity—consider assigning it to groups.

2. One possible way to work through the puzzle:

A. From Clue #1 you know that for every tunnel leading to danger, there is a tunnel that leads to gold. Therefore, the number of tunnels the two combined take up must be even. Given the known tunnels, there are three possibilities:
- 2 Dead End, 3 Gold, 3 Danger
- 4 Dead End, 2 Gold, 2 Danger
- 6 Dead End, 1 Gold, 1 Danger

B. From Clue #2 you know that of the upper four tunnels, two lead to danger (1 in 2 is the same as 2 in 4). Because one of the lower tunnels leads to danger (given), you know that at least 3 tunnels lead to danger. Using the possibilities you narrowed down in #1 above and eliminating ones that no longer can apply, you know that there must be 2 Dead End, 3 Gold, 3 Danger.

C. From Clue #3 you know that one of the four small forks has both tunnels leading to danger. It can't be in the bottom tunnels since there are only three tunnels that lead to danger and you know the upper tunnels have two of them. Besides, you already know that two of the upper tunnels lead to danger;

Hands-On History: Tales & Treasures of the California Gold Rush   Copyright 1995 • Ghost Town Publications • Carmel, California

Teacher's Notes (continued)

therefore, they must be the ones that are paired together on the same fork. In the upper tunnels, the top fork has a given dead end, so it must be the second fork down that has both tunnels leading to danger. Fill those in on the map, and the rest are gold.

Mining for Information (pp. 45-46)
(Mapping the Library's Gold Mine / Mining for Nuggets)

Overview: This activity introduces students to basic library and research skills—how to use a library, where to find information, and how to record information and sources. In Mapping the Library's Gold Mine, they map a fictional library to show where they would find various items and information. Mining for Nuggets is intended to expose students to the wealth of "gold" they can find in a real public library.

Directions for Mapping the Library's Gold Mine

1. Before this activity, discuss how to use libraries and what kinds of things can be found in them. Make sure students understand the general categories/library areas shown on the map of Two Flea Town Library (Library catalog, Reference, Fiction, Nonfiction, etc.).
2. After this activity, discuss the answers students came up with, and compare them with the recommended answers shown in the Answer Key. How did they decide where to look for each item?

Directions for Mining for Nuggets

1. Students can go to a local public library as a class or on their own after school. (Either way, consider pairing students in research teams to encourage brainstorming and cooperative learning.)
2. If a library trip is impractical for your class, you can omit this second part of the activity, or you can devise questions of your own that can be answered with the resources in your school library.
3. Before the library trip, use the mapping exercise in the first part of the activity as a warm-up to a real library trip. Be sure to discuss proper behavior in the library. You may want to contact the local public librarian to explain the activity and arrange convenient hours for students to visit.

Optionally, you can introduce recording and organizing information by having students use 3 x 5-inch index cards to write down each "nugget" of information and its source. What categories might they use to label and organize the cards?
4. After the library trip, have students tell the class what they found *and* the sources they used to find it. Chances are students will have followed different paths to some of the same information, or have come up with different answers to the same question. Use these differences to discuss how to find information most efficiently, creatively, and accurately.

Extension (can be used for either activity)

1. Using the Two Flea Town library map as a takeoff point, make a list of categories of resources (or types of information), and have students draw their own maps of the school or public library showing where to find these resources (information).

Curly Hair Sam's Treasure (pg. 47)

Overview: Students use basic math and map skills to locate a hidden treasure.

Directions

1. Copy pages 47 and 48 back to back for each student.
2. You might want to bring in maps of different areas and scales (e.g., a world map, a USA map, a state map, a county map, a city map) and discuss scale, symbols, legends, etc. either before or after this exercise.

Extensions

1. Have students draw a map showing their route from home to school, including important map elements like scale, symbols, a legend, landmarks, orientation, etc.
2. Have students hide an item on the school grounds and draw a map for another student to find it.
3. Assign different locations around the school for students to draw maps to. Encourage students to include the locations they pass along the way and as many map elements as appropriate—a scale (in paces), symbols, a legend, etc.

As Good As Gold Crossword Puzzle (pp. 49-50)

Overview: A crossword puzzle that highlights "gold" in expressions and stories throughout the ages, in addition to selected Gold Rush facts.

Directions

1. Copy pages 49 and 50 back to back for each student.

Extensions

1. Have students create their own list of expressions and stories that have "gold" as the centerpiece.

Hands-On History: Tales & Treasures of the California Gold Rush   Copyright 1995 • Ghost Town Publications • Carmel, California

DIGGING FOR NUMBERS

1. Fifty feet below the earth's surface is a large layer of gold. You and some friends dig 36 feet straight down the first week. How much deeper do you need to dig before you find the gold? _____

2. You have just found a 5-ounce gold nugget! You hurry to the bank and learn that gold is selling for $8.00 an ounce. How much is your gold nugget worth? _____

3. At the end of a full week of panning you found $28 worth of gold. If you panned exactly the same amount of gold each day, how many dollars worth did you pan each day? _____

4. At the general store you have just bought 2 cans of beans, some tobacco, and a half pound of coffee. If 1 can of beans costs 42 cents, the tobacco costs 75 cents, and 1 pound of coffee costs $1.00, how much did you spend? _____

5. In 1848 about 14,000 people lived in California. By 1852, California's population increased to about 250,000. Approximately how many people flocked into California between 1848 and 1852? _____

6. You don't have much money, but you need to buy a horse. Mrs. Williams, who lives in town, will sell one to you for $11.25. Miner Edward said he would exchange his horse for 3 ounces of gold. If gold is worth $3.50 an ounce, who should you buy the horse from? _____

7. What a gold mine! On your first day of digging you found $150 worth of gold. On the next day, using better tools, you gathered $665, and on the third day you found another $2,000! You were so excited that you spent $120 celebrating with your friends that night. How much did you still have left after your celebration? _____

8. You and 4 friends have struck it rich! Together you found $100 worth of gold in one day, and you want to divide up the gold evenly among you. How much will each person get? _____

9. Use the following chart to answer the next two questions.

Chart of Hours Miner Joe Worked	☁	☁	☀	☀	☀
Day of week	Monday	Tuesday	Wednesday	Thursday	Friday
a.m. hours	4		6	6	6
p.m. hours	5	4	8		8

a. Miner Joe worked a total of 41 hours on the sunny days. How many hours did he work Thursday afternoon? _____

b. Miner Joe worked 7 more hours in the afternoons than he did in the mornings. How many hours did he work Tuesday morning? _____

THE LUCKY MINER MINE

Your Uncle Homer has left a will making you the proud owner of the Lucky Miner Mine. Before he died, Uncle Homer told you that all of the tunnels in the mine end in either a dead end, danger, or gold. But he didn't tell you which tunnels are which, or even how many of each type there are!

Fortunately, Uncle Homer left you a partly finished map of the mine with some mysterious clues scribbled on it. (Uncle Homer was a mathematician before he left for the gold fields, and he loved puzzles.) Can you use Uncle Homer's clues to finish the map and find the tunnels that end in gold?

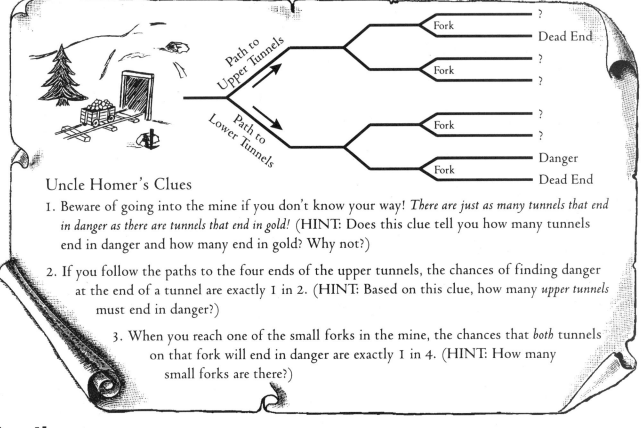

Uncle Homer's Clues

1. Beware of going into the mine if you don't know your way! *There are just as many tunnels that end in danger as there are tunnels that end in gold!* (HINT: Does this clue tell you how many tunnels end in danger and how many end in gold? Why not?)

2. If you follow the paths to the four ends of the upper tunnels, the chances of finding danger at the end of a tunnel are exactly 1 in 2. (HINT: Based on this clue, how many *upper tunnels* must end in danger?)

3. When you reach one of the small forks in the mine, the chances that *both* tunnels on that fork will end in danger are exactly 1 in 4. (HINT: How many small forks are there?)

Directions

Figure out which tunnels have the gold. Use the clues and hints to finish the map and explore the mine safely. Remember, a tunnel can lead to either a *dead end, danger,* or *gold*—these are the *only* three options. Don't give up too soon, but if you need more help, check out the extra hints at the bottom of the page.

☆ **BONUS QUESTION:** There is a mine that has nine tunnels. Four of the tunnels lead to gold, three lead to copper, and two lead to silver. If you walked to the end of only one tunnel, are you more likely to find gold there, or something other than gold?

Extra Hint #1: Based on the map and Clue #1, what is the *most* number of tunnels that could end in danger? (Remember, for every tunnel ending in danger there has to be one that ends in gold.) _____ Now, based on Clue #2, determine how many *upper tunnels* end in danger. (If 1 out of 2 end in danger, then how many out of 4 end in danger?) _____ So, how many total tunnels ending in danger do you now know exist? (Don't forget that you were already given the location of one danger on the map.) _____ If you look at Clue #1 again, how many tunnels ending in gold are there? _____ All you have to do now is figure out which ones are which! If you get stuck, try the next hint.

Extra Hint #2: Based on Clue #3, how many small forks in the mine have both of their two tunnels ending in danger? _____ If you can label these tunnels on the map, you'll be well on your way to finding the gold!

MINING FOR INFORMATION

Did you know that you have a "gold mine" in your own neighborhood or town? Maybe there's one in your own school! This "gold mine" is your school or public library. The information and entertainment that you can find in a library are pure "gold." But as with real gold, you have to know how to look for them!

Mapping the Library's Gold Mine

Try your hand at finishing the "treasure map" of Two Flea Town Library. Where in the library would you go to find each of the following items or information? Write the number of the item in the correct location on the map. (Some locations may have the answers for more than one item. Some locations may not have any of the "gold" you are seeking.)

Where would you go to find . . .

1. An encyclopedia article (for example, an article with general information about gold or a famous person)?

2. Information on whether the library has a certain book? (Imagine that you know the author, the title, the subject, or all three.) HINT: You could ask the librarian, but he or she probably doesn't know the library's collection by heart!

3. A book about minerals written for children?

4. Information on how to use the library?

5. Very current information, such as the price of gold in the United States last week?

6. A map of California during the Gold Rush?

7. A children's book telling about the life of a famous person?

8. The meaning of a word, such as *pyrite*?

9. A current map of the world?

10. The novel *By the Great Horn Spoon* (a story about the Gold Rush for young readers)?

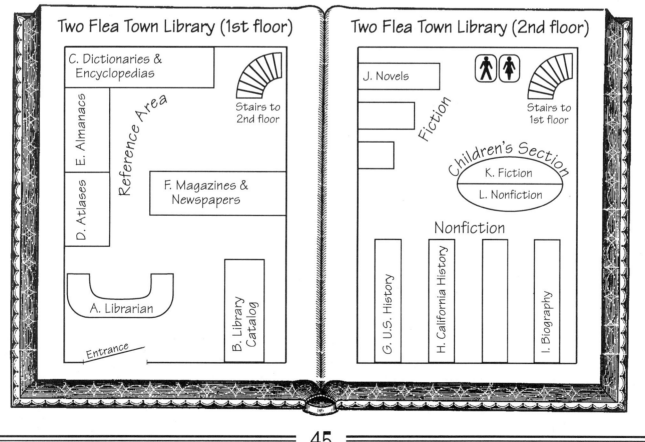

Hands-On History: Tales & Treasures of the California Gold Rush | Copyright 1995 • Ghost Town Publications • Carmel, California

Mining for Nuggets

Go on a treasure hunt through your own public library to find the following "nuggets" of information. For each question, write down *both* the answer *and* the source of your information (the title of the book or publication where you get the information, plus author, if any). Use a separate piece of paper for your answers.

To find the answers, you may need to make your own mental "map" of the library. Remember that sometimes there are many paths to the same information. If you don't find an answer in the first place you look, think of another place to try.

HINT: Use the words and ideas in the question as jumping-off places for your search. For instance, for information about the gold rush mentioned in question 5, you could start by looking for information on "gold," "Yukon," "Klondike," or "Canada." If you get stuck, remember that the librarian is there to guide you!

1. In what country was John Augustus Sutter (the owner of Sutter's Fort) born?

2. About how many miles is it in a straight line from Sutter's home country to California? (HINT: You'll have to figure this one out yourself by locating a map and measuring the distance.)

3. What is the name of the main (child) character in the children's book *By the Great Horn Spoon*?

4. What is the full title of the book about Tom Sawyer written by Mark Twain (also known as Samuel Clemens)?

5. In the late 1800s a second great North American gold rush began in the area of the Klondike and Yukon rivers in northwestern Canada. In approximately what years did this gold rush begin and end?

6. What is fool's gold (pyrite) made of?

7. A *karat* is a measure of how pure a metal is (for example, 18-karat gold is partly gold and partly other metals). How many karats are there in pure gold?

8. The Gold Rush helped to make Sacramento a major city. In what year did Sacramento become the capital of California?

9. During the Gold Rush, the population of California (not counting California Indians) swelled from fewer than 20,000 people to more than 300,000. Approximately how many people live in California today?

10. What was the price of gold (price per ounce) in the United States last week? (HINT: Where would you look for current business information, such as the price of stocks and bonds?)

Hands-On History: Tales & Treasures of the California Gold Rush

CURLY HAIR SAM'S TREASURE

Knowing how to use a map is a very valuable skill. Maps can keep people from getting lost. Maps can also help people to locate unfamiliar places and other things. For example, many hordes of gold that were buried during the California Gold Rush have never been found. If you had a good treasure map, you would know just where to look for these treasures!

Directions

You have received a letter from your dear friend Curly Hair Sam, who headed off to the gold fields of California a year ago. The letter says:

"If you are reading this, something has happened to me. I have hidden my gold carefully, and I want you to have it. Follow the directions and use the map to get my buried riches. Good luck."

You immediately begin the long and difficult journey to the mining camp of Two Flea Town. There you begin your hunt for Curly Hair Sam's treasure.

1. Follow the directions that Curly Hair Sam left you (below). Use the scale to measure the paces you should walk. (HINT: Use a ruler and a pencil to draw your journey on the map.)

2. Answer questions as you come to them.

3. When you have followed all the directions, you will be at the site of the treasure. Write down where you are, and your teacher will tell you if you are correct. Good luck!

Curly Hair Sam's Directions

1. Begin at the center of the Unmarked Grave on the west side of town.

2. Walk east 25 paces. Be careful—many men desire my gold.

3. Walk south 20 paces and turn east. Don't talk to any strangers!

4. Follow the road as it goes east and then southeast. Take your first left. Name the two roads that intersect here: _____ and _____ .

5. Go to the end of this road, go left, and then take your first right. Go 5 paces and stop. When you look west from where you are standing, what kind of building do you see?

_____

6. Careful! Someone may be following you. Just in case, go north 60 paces from where you are standing. Maybe you can lose them.

7. Now, hurry! Cross to the east side of the river using the footbridge to the right of you.

8. Now that you have crossed the bridge, follow the river southeast for 40 paces.

9. Cross the footbridge near you, heading southwest. Now, go 15 paces southwest from the end of the bridge. You are at the beginning of a street. It is _____ Street.

10. In case someone *is* following you, you can lose them in the town. Quickly follow the street until you are just past the hotel. Turn left and go past the saloon on the east side of the street and turn left again. (HINT: Remember which way you are facing before you turn left.)

11. Go 35 paces and stop. Just north of you is where the treasure is buried. It is in the

_____ .

☆ **BONUS QUESTION:** Suppose Juan's pace is a yard, and your pace is 2 feet. When you have each walked 12 paces, how many feet farther has Juan walked? _____

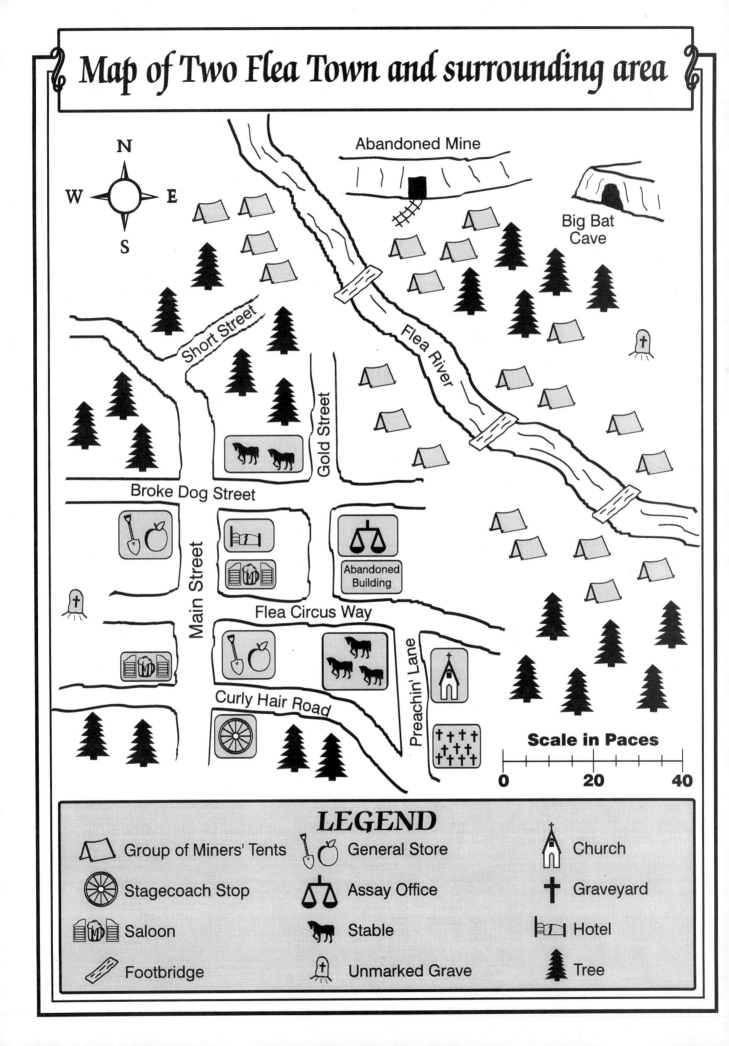

AS GOOD AS GOLD CROSSWORD PUZZLE

Miner's Name: _____

Few words are as magical as "gold." All through history, gold has stood for rare and precious things. Even in ancient times people referred to a fabled period of peace and plenty as the Golden Age. "Treat others as you would have them treat you" is called the Golden Rule. A married couple's fiftieth wedding anniversary is their *golden* anniversary.

The words in this puzzle refer to some of the lore of gold, along with some "nuggets" of information about the California Gold Rush. Can you fill in all the spaces? If so, your work will be "as good as gold!"

The crossword puzzle grid includes the pre-filled answer for 11 Down: SAN FRANCISCO (spelled vertically).

Directions

1. Use the clues to fill in the blank spaces in the puzzle. To solve some of the clues, you might have to do a little "digging" in a dictionary, an encyclopedia, or another book.

2. Write answers in the puzzle without punctuation or blank spaces between words. (See #11 Down, which is already filled in for you.)

3. You don't have to answer the clues in order. Do all the easiest ones first. Where two or more words cross in the puzzle, the letters you've already written in may help you to figure out the missing words. Notice how #11 Down gives you one of the letters for several other words.

As Good As Gold Crossword Puzzle (continued)

Clues

Across

1. Another name for the mineral *pyrite* is _____ _____.

4. The "sickness" caught by people on a rush for gold is called GOLD _____.

5. An athlete at the Olympics can win a GOLD _____.

7. The entrance to the bay near the city named in #11 Down is called the GOLDEN _____.

9. An older name for the city in #11 Down is _____ BUENA.

10. In a famous tale from Greek mythology, everything KING _____ touched turned to gold.

12. California's official state flower is the GOLDEN _____.

13. The full name of the man who hired the man in #15 Across is JOHN _____ SUTTER.

14. The place where the man in #13 Across lived when gold was discovered is called SUTTER'S _____.

15. The man who is credited with finding the gold near Sutter's Mill was _____ MARSHALL.

16. In Greek mythology, the hero Jason led the Argonauts on a quest for the GOLDEN _____.

17. According to an old legend, at the end of a rainbow is a _____ OF GOLD.

18. The location at the tip of South America that many Gold Rush ships passed on their way to California is called CAPE _____.

19. The real name of author Mark Twain was SAMUEL _____.

Down

1. The man named in #15 Across discovered gold near the SOUTH _____ of the American River.

2. The mountain range where much of the Gold Rush took place is called the _____ NEVADA.

3. Gold seekers who took the overland route to California headed _____.

6. A famous bandit of Gold Rush days was named _____ MURRIETA.

7. In an old fable, golden eggs were laid by a _____.

8. The name of Sir Francis Drake's ship was the GOLDEN _____.

11. The northern California village that became a famous city almost overnight during the Gold Rush is known as ____ _____.

16. The golden trout is California's state _____.

17. The Central American country that many gold seekers crossed to get from the Caribbean Sea to the Pacific Ocean is called _____.

Hands-On History: Tales & Treasures of the California Gold Rush   Copyright 1995 ◆ Ghost Town Publications ◆ Carmel, California

The Case of the Telltale Pickle Bottle

A Readers' Theatre Gold Rush Mystery

Teacher's Notes

The following Readers' Theatre script builds on the themes of crime and justice, Gold-Country style, in *Tales and Treasures of the California Gold Rush*. Here are some ideas for using the script in your classroom.

1. Pick a cast, and allow your readers two to four rehearsal sessions. Tell them not to give away the story to other students in the class.

2. Have the cast read the script aloud a few times to master the flow of the sentences before trying to read their lines expressively.

3. Encourage your cast to study the script for clues about the characters' emotions and personalities. Ask them to imagine and discuss what might be going through the characters' minds at each twist and turn of the story.

4. In the last practice or two, encourage expressive reading that brings out the emotions in the script. Encourage the readers to face the audience rather than each other.

5. Have your cast perform the play (with scripts in hand) for the rest of the class. You might want to follow up with additional performances for other classes, or as part of a Gold Rush Jamboree celebration. (See Teacher Talk, page 3.)

6. Create a radio play by audiotaping a performance of the script. If you like, the other students in the class can play the "jury" of miners. They might embellish on the catcalls of Miners 1 and 2 in the script, or even adlib their own as the trial goes on.

7. Use Readers' Theatre as a warmup to the Miners' Court activity (page 32).

8. A performance note: Miner 1 and Miner 2 represent members of the "jury." While the rest of the cast give their lines standing in front of the audience, these two characters could be seated in the audience and call out their lines from there.

The Case of the Telltale Pickle Bottle

CAST OF CHARACTERS

Flea Bailey
Big Ben Blowhard
Joe Greenhorn
Miner 1
Miner 2
Miss Lottie Peartree
Matthew Skinflint
Judge Roy Stringbean

FLEA BAILEY
(speaking to audience)

Allow me to introduce myself. I'm Flea Bailey, attorney at law. Or I should say I *was* an attorney. That was before I ran off to seek my fortune in the great California Gold Rush of 1849. The funny thing is, I had barely arrived in the gold fields when I stumbled onto my most amazing case. I call it the Case of the Telltale Pickle Bottle.

It happened in one of the little mining camps in the Sierra Nevada. In the early days of the Gold Rush, there were no police or judges in those camps. The miners and prospectors made their own rules, and they handled troublemakers in any way they saw fit. Often they just strung 'em up from the nearest tree!

That was the fate facing Joe Greenhorn back in '49. Like me, Greenhorn was a newcomer in the area, and he was accused of a terrible crime. When I arrived in the camp, the local miners were gathering to hear his trial. A tough prospector by the name of Roy Stringbean was elected to act as the judge. I got to the meeting place just as Judge Roy was calling the miners' court to order. . . .

JUDGE ROY

All right, all right, settle down, men! Let's get this hanging party started. I guess you all know the facts of this case. Two nights ago Old Man Hawkins was found in his cabin—strangled to death! I know Hawkins was a mean and stingy old bird. But even he didn't deserve to go to his eternal rest with his neck twisted like a chicken's!

Hands-On History: Tales & Treasures of the California Gold Rush   Copyright 1995 ♦ Ghost Town Publications ♦ Carmel, California

Joe Greenhorn is accused of committing this awful crime. Your job is to hear the evidence and decide whether he's guilty. The whole thing shouldn't take more than twenty minutes—thirty, if you count the hanging. Then we can all get back to finding gold.

Now, I don't want anybody saying that a man doesn't get a fair hearing in this camp. So we're going to do things nice and proper. Big Ben Blowhard is going to be the prosecutor of this case. That means he's going to call witnesses and ask them questions. Then Greenhorn will have a chance to tell his side. After that we can get on with the hanging. Okay, Ben, call your first witness.

BIG BEN   Matthew Skinflint, step forward, please.

JUDGE ROY   'Morning, Matt. Do you solemnly swear to tell the truth about the matter before this court?

MATTHEW   Why, sure, Roy—I mean, Judge. I'm as honest as the day is long. Everybody knows that.

MINER #1   Except when you're puttin' prices on the junk in your general store!

BIG BEN   Matt, tell the good men of the jury exactly what happened last Wednesday evening.

MATTHEW   Well, around eight o'clock I was taking some bottles of pickles to Old Man Hawkins' cabin, down the road from the camp. See, he ordered some from my store a while back, but I was out of stock. So when they came in, I decided to deliver them personally. I was just doing a favor—you know, for a good customer.

MINER #2   You mean you needed some gold dust for the card games, don't you, Matt?

MINER #1   Yeah, I never knew Matt Skinflint to go out of his way for anything except a dollar!

BIG BEN   Let him tell his story, men. So you were taking Old Man Hawkins some bottles of pickles. What happened when you got near the cabin?

MATTHEW   I tell you, men, it was the most awful thing I ever saw. The cabin was very dark—not a lamp or candle burning anywhere. That made me stop and think. Many's the time I've seen old Hawkins burning the midnight oil—probably counting his gold! Suddenly I heard a sound like bottles being smashed.

Luckily, the full moon was just rising over the hills, and the moonlight was slanting through the cabin windows. That's how I saw the old man's body through the open door. He was crumpled on the floor with his head all twisted to one side. And then I saw *him*—Joe Greenhorn—taking the cabin apart like he was searching for something!

JOE That's a lie! I found Uncle lying on the floor when I got there, and the cabin was already all torn up!

BIG BEN So you admit that you were there?

JOE Well, sure, but I didn't kill anybody!

JUDGE ROY The jury will decide that, Greenhorn! Go on, Matt.

MATTHEW Well, it didn't take too many brains to figure out what happened. I knew Greenhorn had murdered the old man. Everybody says Hawkins had a bunch of gold stashed away somewhere, and I figured it was the gold that Greenhorn was after. Anyway, I got nervous watching him. So I crawled away, real quiet-like. After that I hurried back to the camp to get help.

BIG BEN I can take it from there, Judge. Matt ran up and told a bunch of us about finding the body and seeing Greenhorn in the cabin. We all hightailed it to Greenhorn's tent. We found him inside, packing like he was in a big hurry to leave the camp!

Some of us held him down while the others searched through his things. In his saddlebag we found something strange—a pickle bottle with a little gold dust in the bottom!

JOE You're all lying! I don't know anything about any pickle bottles!

BIG BEN My next witness can prove who's lying, Judge—and prove the motive for this terrible crime besides! I now call Miss Lottie Peartree!

JOE Not you, too, Lottie!

LOTTIE Joe, I don't know anything about this, I promise!

BIG BEN I'm sure everyone here knows Miss Lottie Peartree. She's the owner of the prettiest singing voice in all the Gold Country. We're mighty honored to have your traveling show in our camp, Miss Lottie. Now, I know you're friendly with Joe Greenhorn. But I must insist that you tell this court the truth. At about five o'clock on Wednesday afternoon, were you in Matt Skinflint's general store?

LOTTIE Why . . . yes. I was buying some hardtack and coffee.

BIG BEN And at that time did you hear Joe Greenhorn and his uncle having an argument? More especially, did you overhear Old Man Hawkins yell something about pickle bottles?

LOTTIE Yes, but it didn't make any sense.

JUDGE ROY Just tell us exactly what you heard, Miss Lottie.

LOTTIE	Well . . . Old Man Hawkins shouted something about how Joe wasn't going to get his hands on his pickle bottles, and then he stomped out. It sounded crazy to me—and it sounded crazy to Joe, too. I know that, because we talked about it a long while afterward.
BIG BEN	We're not interested in what sounds crazy to you, Miss Lottie. We're only interested in the facts. And the fact is, this argument over pickle bottles happened just a few hours before Joe Greenhorn was seen searching the dead man's cabin—with smashed bottles strewn on the floor!
JUDGE ROY	Maybe I'm a bit slow, but what is all this fuss about pickle bottles?
MATTHEW	I can answer that, Judge. See, I often wondered why Old Man Hawkins kept ordering more pickles from my store. It seemed like the richer he got, the more he craved pickles. Well, the bottle we found in Greenhorn's saddlebag tells the story. Hawkins must have been using those bottles to hide his gold in. That's why Greenhorn was smashing bottles in the cabin. He was looking for the ones that held the gold! I guess he found 'em, too. He must have hidden the rest of 'em someplace before we caught up with him.
BIG BEN	Judge Roy and men of the jury, the case is clear. Joe Greenhorn came to this camp for one purpose. He wanted to get his hands on his uncle's gold—the gold Old Man Hawkins was hiding in pickle bottles! What more proof do we need than the bottle in Greenhorn's saddlebag—with gold dust still in it? Men, I don't know what happened to the rest of that pickled gold. But one thing I know for sure—Joe Greenhorn murdered Old Man Hawkins!
MINER #1	That's the way to tell it, Ben!
MINER #2	What are we waiting for? Let's get the noose!
JUDGE ROY	Hold on, men! Joe Greenhorn, we have more than enough evidence to hang you right here and now. Do you have anything to say for yourself?
JOE	I already told you everything I know, Judge. After I found Uncle's body, I was scared that somebody would think I killed him. I know how you feel about strangers around here. That's why I was getting ready to leave the camp. I'm ashamed now that I left Uncle's body lying there, but that's what I did. So maybe I'm a coward, but I'm no killer. I don't know how that pickle bottle got in my saddlebag. I never saw it before in my life. Oh, what's the use? None of you will believe a word I say!
MINER #2	Why should we? You aren't even smart enough to make up a good alibi!

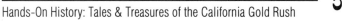

Hands-On History: Tales & Treasures of the California Gold Rush

LOTTIE	You men don't understand! Joe would never do such a thing—I know he wouldn't! I believe you, Joe!
JUDGE ROY	You may be the only one who does, Miss Lottie. Well, what do you say, men? Guilty or not guilty?
MINER #1	Guilty!
MINER #2	Guilty!
JUDGE ROY	Joe Greenhorn, the miners' court has spoken. You have been found guilty of the foul murder of Old Man Hawkins. It is therefore my duty to pronounce sentence upon you. It is now twenty minutes before twelve o'clock. Upon the stroke of noon, you will be taken to the hanging tree outside the camp. There you will be hanged from the neck until you're—
FLEA BAILEY (interrupting)	Just a moment, Your Honor!
JUDGE ROY	"Your Honor"? Hey, I like the sound of that. But who in blazes are you?
FLEA BAILEY	Allow me to introduce myself. I'm Flea Bailey, attorney at law. I hail from the great city of New York. If you'll permit me, Your Honor, I believe I can shed some light on this case.
JUDGE ROY	I don't understand, Mr. Bailey. If you're a newcomer here, what information could you possibly have?
FLEA BAILEY	The same information as you, Your Honor—the information given by the witnesses this morning. Their testimony all points the same way. Joe Greenhorn is innocent!
BIG BEN	Innocent? How can you say that, stranger?
FLEA BAILEY	Your Honor, if I may ask the witnesses a few questions, I believe I can make everything clear.
MINER #2	Aw, get on with it, Roy! These puffed-up Eastern lawyers just like to hear themselves talk.
JUDGE ROY	Maybe so, but I won't have any fancy-dance New Yorker telling people we hang innocent men in this camp. Go ahead and ask your questions, Mr. Bailey. But make it quick. We're all busy men here.
FLEA BAILEY	Thank you, Your Honor. Joe, let me begin with you. What exactly was this argument with your uncle about?

Hands-On History: Tales & Treasures of the California Gold Rush   Copyright 1995 • Ghost Town Publications • Carmel, California

JOE	I don't know, Mr. Bailey. What I mean is, Uncle was a very suspicious man. He was always accusing me of being after his gold. He was going on about that again in the store. Then he began yelling about his pickle bottles. I didn't know what in the world he was talking about.
FLEA BAILEY	And how did you happen to be at your uncle's cabin at around eight o'clock that evening?
JOE	I went there to try to make up with him. I figured he'd have cooled down by then. When I got there, he was cooled down, all right. He was as cold as ice!
FLEA BAILEY	All right, Joe. Your Honor, my next questions are for Miss Lottie Peartree. Just be calm, Miss Lottie, and go on telling the truth. Now, you said that you and Joe talked quite a while after the argument in Mr. Skinflint's store. How long were the two of you together?
LOTTIE	Well, first we went for a walk. Then we had supper around a campfire some men had built. That was right around sunset, I remember—about six o'clock. After supper we talked until it got dark. Then Joe said he was going to his uncle's cabin to try to put things right. That must have been sometime after seven-thirty.
BIG BEN	That's just enough time for Greenhorn to get to the cabin and murder the old man before Matt got there! You're tying the noose around Greenhorn's neck, Mr. Fancy New York Lawyer!
FLEA BAILEY	Let's see if we can untie it, then. Lottie, I'm curious about something else. How did Ben Blowhard know about your overhearing the argument between Joe and his uncle? Did you tell him?
LOTTIE	Why, no, I didn't.
FLEA BAILEY	Was there anyone else in the store at the time?
LOTTIE	No, I don't think so—except for Mr. Skinflint, of course. He was right at the door as I came in. He was sweeping and getting ready to close the shop.
FLEA BAILEY	In other words, Mr. Skinflint could hear Old Man Hawkins yelling about pickle bottles, too. No doubt he's the one who told Mr. Blowhard all about it. Thank you, Miss Lottie. You've been most helpful. Your Honor, that brings me to my most important witness—Matthew Skinflint!
MATTHEW	I already said everything I have to say.
FLEA BAILEY	I only want to clear up a few details of your story, Mr. Skinflint. Is it true that you heard Old Man Hawkins yelling about pickle bottles on Wednesday afternoon?

Hands-On History: Tales & Treasures of the California Gold Rush   Copyright 1995 • Ghost Town Publications • Carmel, California

MATTHEW	What if I did? I didn't know then that the old buzzard was using them to stash his gold in.
FLEA BAILEY	And then sometime toward eight o'clock that night, you went to his cabin to deliver more pickles?
MATTHEW	That's what I said, isn't it?
FLEA BAILEY	And it was mighty thoughtful of you, I'm sure. Someone might wonder why he didn't take his pickles home himself when he was in the store a few hours earlier—but never mind. By the way, are you absolutely positive that you went to the cabin at about eight o'clock?
MATTHEW	Sure I am. I'd already had my supper, and it was dark out—except for the moon, I mean.
FLEA BAILEY	Ah, yes, the moon. That sure was a lucky thing about the full moon rising, wasn't it? Without the moonlight slanting through the windows, you wouldn't have seen a thing inside the cabin. Isn't that right?
MATTHEW	How many times do I have to say it? The moon was just coming up over the hills and shining through the windows. That's how I could see Old Man Hawkins' body through the door—and Joe Greenhorn ransacking the place!
FLEA BAILEY	I guess it's a good thing it wasn't an hour or two later, when the moon was higher in the sky. Then you wouldn't have been able to see into the cabin at all.
MATTHEW	Like you said, it was a lucky thing.
FLEA BAILEY	It certainly was. Mr. Skinflint, I don't suppose you ever give much thought to astronomy, do you?
MATTHEW	Astrono-what?
FLEA BAILEY	Astronomy—you know, the study of the sky. I say this because you seem unaware of a simple astronomical fact—namely, that a full moon *always rises exactly at sunset.* That's around six o'clock at this time of year, Mr. Skinflint—*two hours before* you saw Joe Greenhorn at his uncle's cabin. By eight o'clock the full moon *could not* have been just rising. It was already getting high in the sky—too high to shine through the cabin windows!
MINER #1	By golly, he's right. A full moon does always rise at sunset!
MATTHEW	So maybe I made a mistake about the moon. So what? I know what I saw.
FLEA BAILEY	Oh, I'm sure you do, Mr. Skinflint. I can easily imagine why that pretty picture of the rising moon stuck in your mind's

Hands-On History: Tales & Treasures of the California Gold Rush   Copyright 1995 ◆ Ghost Town Publications ◆ Carmel, California

eye. It's because the moon *was* on the rise and shining through the cabin windows *two hours earlier*, when Old Man Hawkins was strangled!

MATTHEW   Wait a second. Just what are you saying?

FLEA BAILEY   I'm saying that you described the murder scene perfectly, Mr. Skinflint—except for the *time*. Oh, and one other detail—that it wasn't Joe Greenhorn who murdered Old Man Hawkins and searched his cabin by the light of the rising moon. It was you!

MATTHEW   That's a stinking lie! Roy, why are you letting this smart-talking lawyer confuse everything? We already know who killed Old Man Hawkins!

FLEA BAILEY   Do we? I think we know a *story*, Mr. Skinflint. But I know a better one. My story begins at about five o'clock Wednesday afternoon, when you overhear an argument in your store about pickle bottles. Suddenly something clicks into place. For the very first time, you understand what Old Man Hawkins wanted with all those pickles he was always buying from you. He was hiding his gold in the bottles!

Now that you know his secret, you head out to his cabin shortly after closing up shop. That would be right around sunset, I reckon—when the full moon is about to rise. Maybe you only intend to rob the old man. But anyway you wind up in a deadly fight. Before you know it, your hands are gripping his neck. And then he slumps to the floor—dead!

MATTHEW   I don't believe I'm hearing this! Men, don't listen to this claptrap!

FLEA BAILEY   I can picture what happens next, too—because you described it yourself! With the help of the moonlight streaming through the windows, you start tearing up the cabin and smashing bottles until you find what you're looking for—the bottles holding Old Man Hawkins' gold!

Clutching the precious bottles, you hurry back to your shop. But something makes you return to the cabin. I'm guessing that you want to cover up the reason for the murder by cleaning up the broken bottles and replacing them with new ones from your store. So maybe you really were delivering pickles to Old Man Hawkins that night, just as you said—*after* he was already dead!

MATTHEW   And I suppose you can tell me everything else I did that night, can't you? And maybe all of last week while you're at it!

FLEA BAILEY   I don't know about last week, but I have a pretty good idea about Wednesday night. When you get back to the cabin, it's nearly eight o'clock. Now the moon is high in the sky. By its light, you get a nasty surprise. You see Joe Greenhorn about to enter the darkened cabin, where he will find his uncle's body and the smashed bottles. What happens if Joe figures out that you overheard Old Man Hawkins yelling about pickle bottles that afternoon? He just might put two and two together—and then you'll *really* be in a pickle!

It might even cross your mind to kill Joe Greenhorn, too—except that suddenly you think of a better plan, a plan to frame him for the murder!

MATTHEW

Stop this nonsense, Roy! Can't you see he's just making up this whole wild tale to stall for time?

JUDGE ROY

That may be, Matt, but I'm getting kind of interested in hearing how this tale turns out.

MINER #1

Me, too!

MINER #2

Yeah, let him finish, Roy!

FLEA BAILEY

The story's nearly done, Mr. Skinflint. After spotting Joe Greenhorn, you have just enough time to hurry back to camp. You plant one of the stolen bottles in his saddlebag, with a bit of gold dust in the bottom to cinch the frame-up. Then you cry murder so that Joe will be caught, red-handed! It's a perfect frame-up, because *you* know for a fact that Joe has no alibi for eight o'clock. He's as good as hung as long no one discovers that the murder *really* happened around sunset—when Joe was having supper with Miss Lottie Peartree!

MATTHEW

I got to hand it to you, mister. That's some tall tale! But you can't prove a word of it, because it isn't so! It was Joe Greenhorn that killed Old Man Hawkins. Why don't you ask him where he hid the gold? You sure won't find it on me!

FLEA BAILEY

No, not *on* you, Mr. Skinflint—even *you* aren't that dumb! But if you *did* find Old Man Hawkins' gold Wednesday night, you had to stash it somewhere, and do it fast. Chances are it's still where you left it.

Your Honor, I'll bet fifty dollars in solid gold that Old Man Hawkins' pickle bottles can be found where only Matthew Skinflint could have put them—a place that was easy for him to get to in a hurry! And I think I know the perfect hiding place.

How about it, Mr. Skinflint? Do you want to come clean, or shall we search your shop right now—*especially the shelves where you keep your bottled pickles*?

MATTHEW

Why, you fast-talking, belly-crawling son of a snake! I'll strangle *you* next!

JUDGE ROY

Grab him, men! Hold onto him! That's it! Now somebody fetch some rope to tie him up!

MINER #2

String him up is more like it!

JUDGE ROY

Ben, take a couple of men and go on out to Matt's store. Bring back all the pickle bottles you can find. But I think we already know what's in 'em—and it isn't just pickles!

Joe Greenhorn, I guess we owe you an apology. I don't suppose there's any way to make things up to you. But I imagine there will be reward enough in those bottles. After all, you're Old Man Hawkins' nearest relative, so you stand to inherit his property.

LOTTIE   I knew you couldn't have done it, Joe!

JOE   Gosh, Mr. Bailey, I don't know to thank you. I could just about feel the noose tightening around my neck!

LOTTIE   It was awfully clever of you to figure out that business about the moon rising, Mr. Bailey.

FLEA BAILEY   Oh, that isn't what gave Skinflint away, Miss Lottie. I nearly missed that detail myself!

LOTTIE   Then how did you know he was lying?

FLEA BAILEY   Why, it was that pickle bottle the men found in Joe's saddlebag. If Joe really were the killer, I couldn't figure out why he would hang onto a nearly empty bottle—especially if it could tie him to the scene of the crime!

No, the bottle had to have been planted. And when I realized that Skinflint was lying about the moonrise, it all fell into place.

You see, it was Matthew Skinflint's greed that tripped him up. It was out of greed that he murdered Old Man Hawkins. And as badly as he wanted to frame Joe for the murder, he was just so plumb *greedy* that he couldn't stand to leave more than a few bits of gold dust in that telltale bottle!

Hands-On History: Tales & Treasures of the California Gold Rush   Copyright 1995 • Ghost Town Publications • Carmel, California

MORE GOLD NUGGETS

Use these "Gold Nuggets," in addition to the ones scattered throughout the activities, to supplement your Gold Rush lectures.

Gold Facts

◇ Gold melts at about 1,947 degrees Fahrenheit. The boiling point of gold is well above 5,000 degrees Fahrenheit. (Water boils at 212 degrees Fahrenheit.) Its atomic number is 79 and its symbol is Au.

◇ One million pounds of ordinary sea water can contain as much as 2½ pounds of gold! Conservative estimates say that the world's oceans could contain as much as 70 million tons of gold. (Unfortunately, separating out the gold from sea water would cost more than the gold would be worth.)

◇ In 1994 the Galeras volcano in the Columbian Andes was found to be spewing over a pound of gold a day into the atmosphere. It was also leaving 45 pounds of gold a year in the rocks which line its crater.

◇ Gold, 19.3 times heavier than water, is very dense. In fact, a cubic foot of gold weighs over half a ton.

◇ The record price for gold is $880 per ounce, set in January, 1980.

◇ Chemistry, as we know it today, slowly evolved from the work of alchemists in the Middle Ages who tried to make gold from base metals like lead and copper.

◇ Since gold does not tarnish or rust, ornaments of gold which are found in ancient tombs shine as brightly today as they did when they were first placed there.

The California Gold Rush

◇ The Calaveras Nugget, found at the Carson Hill diggings in 1854, weighed 162 pounds!

◇ The mining camp of Volcano produced as much as $500 in a single gold pan, while at the camp of Rich Bar it was fairly common for a single pan to contain $1,500 to $2,000 worth of gold in its dirt.

◇ It is estimated that by 1859 there were 5,000 miles of the flumes and ditches that transported water to the hydraulic mining sites throughout California's Gold Country.

Gold in History

◇ King Tutankhamen was found mummified inside a series of cases (coffins) which fit inside one another. The innermost coffin was of solid gold, and it weighed over a ton!

◇ Gold, a major influence throughout history, has been a driving force in many wars. Both Alexander the Great and Julius Caesar led campaigns motivated by the desire for gold. Many of

Mark Twain's tall tale about a "celebrated jumping frog" is a Gold Rush era story which brought fame to California's Calaveras County. But sometimes truth is just as strange as fiction! Did you know that . . .

◇ A frog's long legs are like springs that help it to escape from other animals?

◇ A Southern Cricket frog is less than 1 inch long but can jump 3 feet?

◇ A North American leopard frog jumps more than 5 feet?

the early explorers, such as Christopher Columbus, Ferdinand Magellan, and Vasco da Gama were inspired in their voyages by the quest for gold.

✧ Long before the Gold Rush, "gold fever" was one of the main reasons the Spanish invaded the New World. But gold wasn't so special to some of the people who were already living there. In fact, when Christopher Columbus reached the New World, he was astonished to see some of the native people using fishhooks made of gold!

Gold Today

✧ The amount of steel produced in one day in the United States is more than twice as great as *all* the gold taken from the Earth in the last 500 years!

✧ The most common use of gold in the United States is in jewelry and arts. The second most common use is in electronics. (Gold is an excellent conductor of electricity, and it is used when corrosion from sparking, arcing, heat, or rust is a problem.) The third most common use is in dentistry.

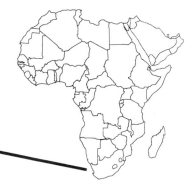

✧ Today, the mines of South Africa produce about 35% of the gold that is mined each year.

✧ The United States consumes (manufacturing, jewelry, etc.) over twice as much gold a year than it produces.

✧ In the 20th century the cyclotron and other particle accelerators have made tiny particles of gold from other metals.

Things That Are Rare . . .

Have you ever heard of a comic book made of gold? How about a baseball card or a game board? Even if they aren't really made out of gold, some old objects are worth a lot of money simply because (like gold) they are rare. Would you believe that . . .

✧ A 1939 *Batman* comic book was sold to a collector in 1991 for $55,000?

✧ An early baseball card with the picture of old-time star Honus Wagner was sold for $18,000 in the 1990s?

✧ The original, hand-made board for the game *Monopoly* (dating from the 1930s) sold in 1992 for $71,500?

Who knows? Maybe an everyday object in the home of one of your students will prove to be a "buried treasure" years from now!

Hands-On History: Tales & Treasures of the California Gold Rush   Copyright 1995 • Ghost Town Publications • Carmel, California

Answer Key

Where in the World Did I Come From? (pg. 9)

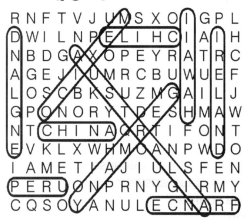

1. China
2. Germany
3. Chile
4. Australia
5. England
6. Ireland
7. Peru
8. Hawaii
9. France
10. Mexico

Westward Journey Word Match (pg. 10)

1. spring (F)
2. Cape Horn (Q)
3. 1500 (B)
4. cholera (E)
5. Sierra Nevada (A)
6. 6 (G)
7. Independence (L)
8. salt (S)
9. Caribbean (P)
10. oxen (C)

Betcha Can'ts (pp. 13-14)

NOTE: A * indicates answers will vary.
1. Richard Barter / Pirate / A mule is a cross between a horse and a donkey (ass). (all 3 = 10 pts.)
2. * (5 pts)
3. The U.S. Gold Bullion Depository is located there. (10 pts)
4. 100 miles (10 pts) / 2½ hours (5 pts)
5. * (5 pts) / * (5 pts)
6. 5 grams (5 pts) / 400 nickels (10 pts)
7. Brass (primarily copper and zinc) / bronze (primarily copper and tin) (need both = 10 pts)
8. ½ cubic yard (5 pts) / 2½ cubic yards (5 pts)
9. * (make sure covers "four w's") (15 pts)

How Did They Get That Gold? (pg. 15)

Answers to these questions may vary slightly.
1. Answers may include: Coyote Hole, Long Tom/Sluice, Panning, Rocker/Cradle, Hydraulic Mining
2. Lode deposits are still beneath the Earth's surface while placer deposits have already reached the surface through erosion.
3. Hydraulic mining
4. Gunpowder, picks, shovels
5. Panning
6. Holes often caved in.
7. Ridges
Bonus Question: Hydraulic mining and quartz mining (usually)

How Did They Get That Gold? (pg. 16)

1. Coyote / bedrock / placer
2. Lode / quartz
3. Hydraulic mining
4. Panning
5. Rockers / soil (or similar word)
6. Tom / water / ridges (or riffles)
7. 8 / settle (or similar word)

Edit This Newspaper (pg. 40)

Siera (1)	Sierra (L)
east (1)	west (F)
Atlantic (1)	Pacific (F)
Missourri (1)	Missouri (L)
Chili (2)	Chile (L)
German (2)	French (F)
1849 (3)	1848 (F)
bilding (3)	building (L)
fort (3)	mill or sawmill (F)